Basics of Branding

Basics of Branding

A Practical Guide for Managers

Jay Gronlund

First published in 2013 by
Business Expert Press, LLC
222 East 46th Street, New York, NY 10017
www.businessexpertpress.com

ISBN-13: 978-1-60649-592-6 (paperback)
ISBN-13: 978-1-60649-593-3 (e-book)

Business Expert Press Marketing Strategy collection

Collection ISSN: 2150-9654 (print)
Collection ISSN: 2150-9662 (electronic)

Cover and interior design by Exeter Premedia Services Private Ltd., Chennai, India

First edition: 2013

10 9 8 7 6 5 4 3 2 1

Printed in the United States of America.

Abstract

Smart branding is essential for success, yet it is often misunderstood. Developing a brand that is relevant, distinct, and emotionally compelling can be very difficult for many managers, mainly because they don't realize exactly what and how much goes into this branding process. This book will explain this process.

Branding is all about creating a message or an impression that makes an impact and creates a rational and emotional connection with a customer. Forming a bond of trust and comfort will build brand equity (i.e., how people value your brand) and customer loyalty. A strong brand positioning should be the heart of all customer-centric initiatives (e.g., marketing, sales, public relations, IT, customer services); it must provide clear direction for communicating a consistent, focused message that will capture the minds and hearts of target customers.

Emphasizing these basics of branding is important for all managers, but in different ways. We are living in a dynamic, transformative global economy with mind-boggling advances in technology. Managers today can easily become preoccupied with social media vehicles and the innovative features of electronic devices, and hence neglect the importance of the content or the message. This book will bring them back to the fundamentals, to develop a value proposition that will excite customers.

Managers in the B2C world will find this book refreshingly practical. Adhering to the core elements of positioning and branding will help them develop more emotionally rich and powerful content. B2B managers will better understand and discover the real value of good branding so that their marketing and sales communications will go beyond product features and emphasize relevant benefits that will strengthen their relationships with targeted customers. Senior executives of every type of company will gain a new strategic perspective that will enable them to build a more captivated, loyal customer base. Finally, students of marketing can build a firm foundation to apply these basics of branding in both digital and traditional communications.

Keywords

basics of branding, positioning statement, emotional branding, consumer insights, corporate branding, global branding, country branding, market research, creativity, ideation, innovation model, brand names and logos, B2B, business-to-business, value proposition, value pricing, commoditization, marketing and sales alignment, silos, brand trust, social media, brand architecture, personal branding, employer branding, brand equity, B2C, business-to-consumer.

Contents

Preface

Why Branding Is Even More Important Today

This book is about changing people's attitudes and behavior. It deals with the fundamentals of communication and persuasion, and also with messaging that can change how people think. I wrote this book to help managers re-discover critical principles of marketing that are so often lost or misunderstood in today's world of fast-paced communications and information clutter. And the core of marketing is branding.

The role of marketing in business continues to fluctuate along with the moods of the economy, advances in technology, and the ever-changing fickleness of consumers. "Mad Men" reminds us of the dominance of ad agencies between the 1950s and 1970s, especially the prevalent use of print advertising. Fast forward to today, and it is obvious how much the world of mass marketing has transformed to one-on-one, interactive communications in this current age of the internet. Competition in most industries is more intense than ever. We live in a world of product clutter, overloaded with information from so many sources, plus technological innovations dramatically changing our behavior and lifestyles, especially the younger generations (Z and Y). Anyone under 30 today can multitask and adapt with such speed and efficiency that still astounds older adults.

Most business managers don't really understand "branding." They usually think this discipline starts with a new, catchy name and then they become fixated with all the media and digital options that exist today. What is lacking in both B2B and B2C circles is the strategic side of branding—that is, the creativity, customer research, and competitive assessments, matched against a realistic examination of a company's strengths and ability to deliver on promises. This involves more thorough research and due diligence than ever. Understanding your customers more fully is essential to determine the optimal positioning for creating "content" or a message that will truly resonate with them. This must include a credible benefit or promise to the target customer (i.e., its "added value") to make a brand genuinely relevant and stand out in today's overcrowded, fast-paced world. (Note: The terms "consumers," used mainly in packaged-goods marketing, and "customers," traditionally referring to the trade in consumer marketing and more universally used in B2B marketing, are used interchangeably in this book to minimize confusion and focus attention on the main applications of these basic branding principles.)

This book on the "Basics of Branding" reflects my personal experience of over 40 years in all aspects of marketing (B2C, B2B, global, and especially in new business development) and my teaching a course on "Positioning and Brand Development" at NYU since 1999. It is designed to refocus the attention of all business managers on these fundamental building blocks for successful brand development and successful marketing. It emphasizes the core principles that will enable people to view and use branding as a tool for a variety of purposes (e.g., corporate and product branding, personal branding, global branding, country branding). It also addresses the challenge of transforming a strategic idea that is often viewed as theoretical, especially in the B2B world, to relevant content, simple messaging, and actionable programs for sales people. The book is basic, practical, and single-mindedly clear, almost like a handbook that will forever be indispensible as a reference guide.

CHAPTER 1

What Is Branding Really About?

A Classic, Ubiquitous Misunderstanding of "Branding"

Branding is hot. You cannot read a newspaper, magazine, or blog these days without coming across some reference to "branding." Branding has indeed become a universal benchmark for something noteworthy or successful. This recognition is certainly warranted. Research from McKinsey & Company supports the importance of good branding, finding that companies with strong brands achieve returns 1.9 times higher than their industry average.

Everyone seems to want to enhance their "brand," do more "branding," or simply "re-brand" these days. However, these terms are usually misused because managers don't really understand the basic concept of "branding." As a result, they miss the real opportunity to distinguish their product or corporate brand.

How many times have we heard statements by executives like "we must start a branding campaign," or "our problem is one of branding," or "branding is only good for consumer goods." What they're really talking about is a communications or marketing execution issue (e.g., building awareness, lead generation initiatives, changing the name, or reaching a wider audience). This is not branding per se. Instead, it is a misconception that distracts from the real opportunity to build their business or resolve a marketing problem.

In a 2010 blog "We've Branded Ourselves to Death," Seth Godin, a reputable marketing blogger, prudently recognized the "glut of brand advertising ... and customers no longer want to be spammed with information about the product or service; they want to feel the connection of it." What he means is that most advertising and even selling initiatives communicate a diatribe of product "features" and do not offer a distinctive value proposition or a focused, compelling benefit. It's called "clutter!"

So What Really Is "Branding"?

It certainly is trendy today to depict anything and everything as a brand. But how can one really apply the concept of branding in a way that practically helps managers when there are so many interpretations of this elusive concept or tool. Yes, it really is a tool, and a valuable one if fully understood and used strategically.

Trying to define a "brand" is similar to the challenge of explaining "charisma." The dictionary defines charisma as "a personal magic of leadership arousing special popular loyalty or enthusiasm for a statesman or military commander." Fine in theory, but I think it is extremely difficult to apply this concept except by use of an analogy. For example, Kennedy had charisma, while Nixon didn't. Many feel the same way about Obama having it, while Romney lacked this quality.

The dictionary definition of a brand is even more elusive: "a mark (made by burning with a hot iron or with a stamp), or a class of goods identified as the product of a single firm or manufacturer." Actually, the word brand comes from the old Norse word, "brandr," meaning to burn, which was how early man stamped his ownership on livestock. Today, a brand also consists of some form of identification, a name and/or some kind of a logo/symbol. But it is what such a name or symbol means to people, which will determine the value and strength of a brand.

In general, marketing can be a challenging discipline because ultimately you are trying to understand and shape human behavior, an extremely complex and unpredictable subject. Learning the basics of branding can be easier if one focuses on the fundamentals, and is not distracted by subtle, subjective interpretations. In particular, marketers can be significantly more productive and innovative if they concentrate on the perceptions of their target customer.

There are many succinct definitions for a "brand"—a promise, an expectation of performance, a reputation, a mark of trust—but a compelling product or corporate brand description should start with a clear positioning, one that strategically addresses the target customers' needs and distinguishes it from competition. Even a company's vision and/or mission statement, and especially its values and brand image, should ideally emanate from the research and analysis that goes into a brand positioning.

Branding is not about one's product offering or marketing effort. It is more about the customer, and how to develop a meaningful relationship with the customer—what is often called the "customer experience." Peter Drucker, a famous business philosopher and author, once said "the purpose of business is not to make money; it is to create a customer and to satisfy that customer."

In their annual report on the most influential brands in the United States, the brand specialist firm, Ipsos, clearly summarized the following important link between brands and people:

> Brands have meaning. Brands have personality. Brands have attitude. And because people so often identify with, relate to, and define themselves by them, brands have influence.

A brand breathes life into a positioning strategy so that customers can naturally trust it, feel comfortable with it, and ultimately be loyal to it. As Seth Godin puts it, branding is not marketing—instead "it should inspire, lead, and tap into the brand's passions so you'll tap into your customers' passion and build a committed following." Zig Ziglar, a famous marketing philosopher, added "people don't buy for logical reasons. They buy for emotional reasons."

These customer-centric principles are essential to understand what branding is really all about. It is a discipline that has many dimensions to it, although there is always a risk that students of branding will try to memorize specific brand definitions instead of understanding these principles and how to develop or use brands as a tool. In any case, here are some succinct explanations of the lexicon of branding found in various textbooks; these are best absorbed within the context of a strategic business development initiative:

- **Brand:** A promise, with relevant benefits. *Wikipedia* defines a brand as "the essence of what will be delivered or experienced."
- **Brand Identity:** Visual expression of a brand, for example, marks like the logo, symbol, and font style.

- **Brand Image:** Collection of impressions of what the brand "looks like," forming a set of perceptions in the customer's mind.
- **Brand Essence:** Summary of the brand's core values and emotions.
- **Brand Character (or Personality):** The personality of the brand with all his/her personality traits and emotions, usually like the target audience or customer.
- **Brand Reputation:** While a brand is related to who you are (e.g., company, product, service, or person), or the emotional and functional experience others have with you, reputation is *how* this experience is interpreted over time.
- **Brand Culture:** System of values that surround the brand.
- **Brand Positioning:** What a brand stands for in the minds of customers, relative to competition and the benefits or promises.
- **Brand Equity:** The total accumulated value or worth of a brand.

In this book, the term "branding" will be discussed in a way that embraces all these various definitions. You will undoubtedly find these or similar definitions used by other business consultants and academicians. Trying to memorize these particular definitions can be a distraction from the real intent of this book, that is, for you to understand the basics of branding so that you can apply these principles to your own business or personal needs. It is far more important to learn how to develop strong brands.

Branding and Marketing

It would be remiss if one does not try to understand "branding" in the context of "marketing," which begs the question—how to accurately and meaningfully define "marketing." While most business people have a good idea of what marketing is all about, many in the B2B world, especially in highly technical industries, tend to be more sales and product driven. Their sense of branding is not nearly as sophisticated or progressive as in the B2C world, although they are becoming more sensitive to the need for stronger corporate and product brands.

Most marketing definitions tend to be more theoretical, and not practical. And they usually don't acknowledge the integral role of branding in their definitions. Some examples of noteworthy definitions of "marketing" demonstrate this (underlining is mine):

> *Marketing is the activity, set of institutions, and process for creating, communicating, delivering, and exchanging offerings that have value to customers, clients, partners, and society at large.*
>
> American Marketing Association

> *Marketing is the social <u>process</u> by which individuals and groups obtain what they <u>need and want</u> through creating and exchanging products and <u>value</u> with others.*
>
> Philip Kotler, famous author of marketing books

> *Marketing is the <u>process</u> used to determine what products or services may be of interest to customers and the strategy to use in sales, <u>communications</u>, and business development. It is an integrated process through which companies build strong customer relationships and create <u>value</u> for their customers and themselves.*
>
> *Wikipedia*

None of these definitions are incorrect. In fact, most share a common element that is important for understanding marketing (see underlining above):

- It is about creating value for customers and companies
- Inherently, it is a process, with an implied discipline
- It is built on identifying and satisfying needs and wants
- Marketing absolutely requires communicating

What is noteworthy, however, are some integral features that are missing from these definitions, which would help one better understand the more meaningful, practical applications of marketing, especially the role that branding plays in this discipline. For example, not one of these definitions included the word "brand," but instead referred to "products" or "services." Also, none are very simple. At its core, "marketing" is ultimately about influencing or causing change in *behavior*. Other critical aspects that should be recognized when trying to understand and apply marketing, which are essential for branding, include the following:

- Must qualify a target: a predetermined segment of customers
- Must gain a real or perceived advantage over competition
- Success will depend on building brands, not products or offers

The founders of Business Development Network, Richard Czerniawski and Michael Maloney, offer a definition that is more target specific, behavioral, competitive, and brand driven, which I personally favor:

Marketing is the art and science of influencing—through the establishment of a valued relationship—a pre-determined set of target customers to prefer and choose one's brand over the competition.

Branding and Positioning

No one can appreciate the usefulness of branding as a tool without first understanding how it relates to the strategic process of positioning. From the standpoint of a proactive marketer, positioning is how one describes something (e.g., a product service, organization, individual, country, event) so that your audience will distinguish it from competition in terms of how it fits a compelling and relevant need. Or from the customer's perspective, how you want your audience to perceive and feel about your product/service.

The brand is an extension of the positioning, the "net impression" or essence of what the positioning means to its audience. What makes a brand so vital is that it is the basis for an emotional bond between the customer and this special meaning of the product. The key is the *relationship*. The brand brings the positioning to life, so it becomes easier for a person to perceive and feel more attached to an appealing brand.

It is simple human nature for people to respond more strongly to other people—the "chemistry" between people, rather than the main qualities of a "thing"—for example, a product or service. This is why it is helpful for one to think of a brand as a human "personality" (other common descriptors include brand character, identity, image, and soul).

Webster's concise definition of personality is perfect for understanding how a brand personality should be described: "Individuality, distinctive personal qualities." A brand should create an impression that reflects the complexion, temperament, and spirit of a personality, the brand personality. The relevance and appeal of these special personal qualities will also determine the perceived value of the brand. The personality will often mirror the profile of the primary user as well. These meaningful personality qualities will form the basis of a relationship, ideally based on emotions and feelings, between the brand and the customer. Examples of concise brand personality descriptions are as follows:

Pepsi: Active, fun, young at heart, outrageous—everything a young person would aspire to be

Nike: Competitive, leader, positive role model, genuine, likeable, gentleman—like Michael Jordan

Product Positioning Versus Brand Positioning

It is important to also recognize the difference between product positioning and brand positioning. The former focuses on what a product does on a functional or basic level. In the pharmaceutical industry, for instance, such a product positioning simply describes the indication (functional role) of a special compound. A true brand positioning describes the entire offering, encompassing both the tangible and the intangible elements to create a genuine experience and an emotional connection between the brand and the customer. This relationship should build over time as marketing continues to reinforce these important intangibles in different forms and media. For example, every time a customer has a Starbucks experience, he or she is exposed to an array of innovative offers that solidify a unique brand impression of being "novel, hip, and cool." There are other characteristics that demonstrate how good brand positioning can ideally become more enduring:

- **Mirrors Its Customers:** It is critical for the customer to identify with the brand. A Mac is more than a mobile computer to its loyalists; it empowers them to sustain their passions.

- **Shows a Distinct Personality:** While a PC is perceived as traditional and industrial, a Mac is cool and contemporary. Pepsi is somewhat counter cultural compared with Coke, which has a more clean-cut and all-American persona.
- **Leverages Its Culture:** The perception of different cultures can help distinguish and support a special brand image: Mercedes is all German, Coke and McDonald's share their American roots and tastes with the rest of the world, and Perrier and Evian are very French.

Common Threads for Smart Branding

Branding is a term that is definitely over used and/or often used inappropriately. Sure, anything with a name and/or logo by the most minimal definition is technically a "brand." But is it a good brand, something special, meaningful, and adding value for the customer, and hence worthwhile for the manufacturer?

While brands are used to describe so many phenomena today— products, services people, places, events—successful brands do have some common attributes. These are some key ingredients and critical building blocks for good branding:

- **Name:** Whether it's Apple, the Olympics, or your own name, this is the first "touch point" that is exposed to the customer, and therefore will always create a certain impression.
- **A Market Opportunity:** There must be a situation with enough people out there with similar needs to make it worthwhile to go through the strategic process of positioning and branding.
- **Relevant Appeal:** The audience that a brand must address should have certain compelling needs and desires that will dictate how the brand will be shaped.
- **Different:** The world is full of options, so a brand must be able to make a promise and create an impression that it is different in a relevant and credible way from competition, so the customer will prefer your brand.
- **Aspirational:** Ideally, a brand should present a proposition that is emotional, full of hope, and trust. A brand mission expresses the

purpose of a brand in a way that can cause change and achieve the ideal. Examples of some well-known brand missions are as follows:

- **Nike:** Helps athletes maximize performance
- **Hallmark Cards:** Provides people with a high-quality means of communicating emotions
- **Apple:** Builds the computer and other devices ordinary folks can use (original)
- **FedEx:** Provides overnight delivery you can count on

Why Branding Is So Critical Today?

We are living in an age of information overload. New technology has advanced so much that we are constantly inundated with communication messages wherever we go, and the number of options to consider for any purchase decision can be overwhelming these days. With all the clutter today, marketers face the awesome challenge of somehow getting their brand to stand out in this overcrowded world. The number and complexity of consumer choices are increasing all the time, yet the hours in a day and our mental capacities remain the same. Just imagine a consumer standing in front of a specific food or a personal-care product section of a supermarket or pharmacy, trying to quickly absorb the differences among a vast array of product brands and their extended types, shapes, sizes, and packages, and having only minutes to make that purchase decision. We've all been there, or at least witnessed this scenario. It is a truly daunting and frustrating experience.

It would be far easier if this consumer could immediately identify one element in this diverse product section that would give him/her some degree of instant comfort and assurance. Ideally, it should be a brand name that provides immediate recognition and comfort, or maybe a new brand name but from a well-known corporation, or a familiar symbol or logo next to the name, or perhaps the special graphics and colors on the package.

These triggers for instant identification are called "touch points." Whatever the particular touch point is, it should conjure up a positive feeling that implies an expectation of performance or even a promise of a predictable experience, hence a sense of trust. This "brand power" that enables the consumer to make this purchase decision more easily and quickly with reduced risk is why branding is so important today, especially in light of all the clutter that surrounds us.

While we may not be so conscious of the extreme clutter that has filled our daily lives, it is useful to understand the main driving forces behind this overload trend, plus the implications for developing relevant and distinct brands:

- **Advertising:** Exposure to advertising of all forms has become so ubiquitous that it is impossible to spend a day without feeling bombarded with different messages. Mass media is still a mainstay, but communications capabilities are now so sophisticated that narrowly targeted "rifle shot" messages have become more common, whether it is in stores, over television, on the internet, digital apps, or other media vehicles. In 1965, three 60-second commercials could reach 80% of 18–49-year-old women in the United States. Today, this would require over 90 such commercials. Will this constant information overload help one to appreciate the challenge for any particular brand to stand out?

- **Competition:** The intensity of competition, especially with the steady flow of new products/services, is mind boggling today. Everyone is chasing the same goal—to capture an open door to your mind and to make a lasting impression. There is simply not enough brain capacity or memory in our human heads to cope with the vast number of different types of product and service offerings available in this information overload time. Imagine, there are over 15,000 new products introduced each year (3,000 in supermarkets alone), there are about 750 car names to choose from, over 150 brands of lipstick, and the examples can go on and on.

- **Product Distinction:** Because of the extremely competitive nature of most businesses, it has become increasingly difficult to create a meaningful and especially a demonstrable point of difference in most consumer products. In most cases, the basic product function or performance of various products in a given category is very similar. More and more, marketers are relying on packaging design, cosmetic nuances (e.g., color, scent), and even affiliated services to create an impression of being different and to add value.

- **Regulations:** Claims of real superior performance are rare these days. Government and even industry associations are constantly reviewing all advertising and packaging copy, and are very sensitive to comparative claims. Furthermore, such comparisons to other products are considered to be in bad taste in many countries outside the United States. The net result is the risk of several products in some categories being perceived as just "me-too" or commodity brands, which is one of the key reasons for the growth of cheaper generic brands.

- **Credibility:** Today, consumers are more cynical and suspicious of advertising than ever before. The well-publicized incidences of corporate greed and corruption have only aggravated this mind-set. Integrity in marketing is essential today, especially if one wants to develop credible brands and solid consumer loyalty.

Today's Biggest Challenge: CONTENT That Inspires

Even though we are flooded with new digital media options and promotions these days, most marketers seem to be obsessed with simply adding more and more tactical offers or product promises. This is the wrong direction. Instead, more emphasis should be on developing relevant content or a focused message that will reinforce the brand impression and stimulate that desired "WOW" reaction, which will set your company or product apart from the clutter, and may also ensure it is shared and goes viral on digital media. As Chip and Dan Heath write in their recent book *Made to Stick*, the idea behind a brand story or communications must be "sticky"—simple, concrete, credible, and emotional. People don't remember a laundry list of features or an abstract concept. They want to relate to a core idea or brand, become emotionally attached to it, and feel comfortable to act on it—even purchase it.

Developing a focused, compelling brand message is not easy. It takes time, intensive research, independent diverse thinking, and especially an effort to generate new, creative ideas. Ultimately, it must define a corporation, product, or service brand in a way that leads to distinctive, meaningful content, ideally with a "sticky hook" that will break through the clutter, become viral, and eventually result in a purchasing action.

Criteria for Powerful Brands

The strength of a brand is relative. Anything with a name is technically a brand, but how effective it is as a marketing tool depends on the strategic positioning of the brand (i.e., the content) and of course how well it is marketed. A good brand must start with the two main requirements for positioning: filling a customer's need and being different from competition, in reality and at least in perception.

Branding is essentially about developing relationships, and consumers are much more likely to gravitate to a brand if it is perceived more like another human being. In other words, the appeal of a brand is very similar to the mutual attraction between two people, ideally with a trustful, compatible relationship that evolves over time. Like people, brands are complex and should offer many complimentary attributes that help solidify this common bond of friendship. In addition, brand and people relationships take time to develop, and usually become stronger with constant reinforcement of these critical qualities:

- **Benefit or Value Proposition:** At a minimum, a brand positioning must fill a customer's need or desire. It must add value and deliver on its promise to fulfill a basic functional need of the consumer, and the benefit should ideally create an emotional connection based on the consumer's perception, feelings, and expectations.
- **Competitive Advantage:** A strong brand must offer a credible reason for the consumer to select that brand instead of another competing brand. This strategic point of difference can be real or perceived, and the advantage should also be consistently reinforced over the life of a brand.
- **Consistency and Sustainability:** While elements of the positioning may change over time to reflect the dynamics of the market (e.g., competitive changes, new product introductions, evolving consumer desires or motivations), the essence of a brand should never change. Often called the DNA of a brand, this fundamental articulation of what a brand means to a consumer should transcend the physical attributes of the product and endure over time. For example, the brand essence for Kraft's Philadelphia Cream Cheese is described as

"my daily trip to paradise." The brand should provide a consistent face to the consumer.

- **Focus:** The net impression offered by a brand must be simple and focused, communicated in a single-minded way. The best brands create a perception of intangible benefits or an added value that generates a feeling of trust and compassion at a nonrational level.

- **Name and Logo/Symbol:** First impressions are generally lasting impressions. Developing the right name and logo/symbol is crucial for brand success, as it must reflect the brand personality and the expectations and needs of consumers. The more memorable the name and the better the fit, the more likely a brand will ultimately create strong customer loyalty.

- **Business Potential:** In addition to creating an enduring relationship with consumers, strong brands have significant business advantages: higher profitability because one can charge a higher price with less risk, marketing efficiencies, more effective global expansion, and a solid foundation for meaningful line extensions.

Brand is greater than the product

Strategic Positioning for Powerful Brands

Positioning defines how you want your brand to be perceived. It provides a relevant value proposition based on the perception as to why consumers should select your product or service instead of a competitor's. Positioning is analogous to an architect's blueprint for a building, only here it provides the specifications for developing a brand and also the direction for the marketing implementation and action—from new products to all forms of traditional and internet advertising.

Taking this analogy one step further, visualize a city like New York, which is known for its skyscrapers. Each building provides specific services so that it can fulfill the basic needs of its tenants and visitors. But there are some special buildings that have more character and evoke positive, memorable emotions—The Chrysler Building, The Flatiron Building, The Empire State Building, and The Seagram Building. They stand out in people's minds because of their unique design and history. Similarly, the most noteworthy brands are those that have a special design as well. This design process is the positioning process.

Positioning is a strategic discipline that will ultimately establish the most important reason for selecting a brand. It addresses the following three essential business purposes:

1. By identifying the most critical benefit and reasons why your target consumer should prefer your product over the competitor's, it establishes the optimal appeal of the brand so that it can fulfill its maximum potential in the market place.
2. Positioning establishes the strategic vision, consistent with the parent company's vision, and importantly the personality of the brand.
3. It becomes the navigator or directional compass for guiding all marketing development, such as digital and traditional advertising, packaging, pricing, public relations, website design, promotion and merchandising, including ideally new product development.

Summary

While "branding" is becoming more recognized as a vital business tool, it is also misunderstood by many people. Most often, they only think of the brand name or the "look" of the brand. These are important components of a brand, but it is much more than this exterior. Branding is all about creating a distinct, positive impression that will foster a lasting relationship with the target customer, so the basic message and content become the key to successful branding.

Branding is best understood when explained in the context of marketing. Essentially, it is the heart of marketing as all types of marketing and communications initiatives should reflect this core brand positioning.

CHAPTER 2

The Positioning Statement, Emotions, and Brand Equity

A Simple Tool, but a Must for Branding

All good consumer product companies use some form of the positioning statement. This is a critical marketing tool that forces one to summarize in writing the blueprint for a brand. It should be emphasized that a positioning statement is not prepared on a whim or without an enormous effort and time commitment. It should be the culmination of exhaustive market research with consumers, a comprehensive assessment of the market potential and optimal opportunity for a brand, and a thorough analysis of the competition. While most companies have their own customized terminology and format, a positioning statement usually includes the following elements:

Target Customer and Needs

Identifying the primary target audience is perhaps the most important "first step" in marketing. It answers the critical question, "for whom?". Often, a category requires a dual audience, or a primary and secondary segment that should be targeted. This is particularly relevant in the pharmaceutical industry, where the doctor, pharmacist, or both play such a vital role in recommending certain over-the-counter (OTC) or prescription products.

There is an understandable tendency, once a new product has been developed, to simply assume that the products' most distinguishable attributes will become the main basis for trial and usage, especially if it reflects years of research and development. This may eventually be the case, but there is absolutely no substitute for doing the mandatory research that will help define exactly the profile of the target prospect; what his/her needs, values, and desires are; and whether/how a product or service can make a credible and deliverable promise that addresses these needs. Understanding these target audience needs, wants, or expectations requires an extensive examination of the following:

- Current usage habits—where, when, by whom, other circumstances, including competition.
- Intensity of all these needs and wants, in order of priority.
- Perceptions about and attitudes to your product and the competition.
- Relevance of these needs, plus expectations for delivering on promises.
- Trends and changes in consumers' preferences or tastes.
- Overall brand potential, indicated by the incidence of a need or problem, the intensity, and the number of people with similar needs.

In research, consumers will initially express their problems or needs in a rational way, or what they want and how their needs should be fulfilled. These are called *functional* or *physical needs*. For example, I want to stop coughing, or I want the aches and pains in my back to go away. These rational desires are identified "through the head," and address what consumers want a product to do for them in terms of performance. At a minimum, a product must be able to deliver on any of the promises to address these basic functional, conscious needs.

By probing and using other research techniques, experienced marketers will take these needs one step further and discern how consumers want to feel, which reflects their emotional needs ("through the heart"). Identifying these intangible feelings, often called the "sweet spot," should be the real goal of any positioning research, including how consumers actually express their wish for ultimate satisfaction. Typical examples of desired feelings include peace of mind, assurance, sense of trust, feeling safe, and so on.

An example of a success story built on emotional needs is Starbucks. They recognized an emerging trend where more consumers wanted to drink authentic, robust coffee, and were even willing to experiment with more exotic, creative coffee beverages. However, this basic functional need was not be enough to make Starbucks really stand out. They stepped up to address an emotional dimension of this functional customer need, the desire for a special experience. Starbucks positioned their coffee shops as a distinct "coffee-supplemented" experience, where customers could enjoy the "chic European-style" ambience in addition to strong coffee. There were also special features in the original Starbucks café environment that offered a distinctive yet relevant appeal to the unique psyche and desires (classical music, internet access, unique packaging, etc.) of its target customers, who tended to be more urbane, proactive, upscale, sophisticated, and just wanted to "chill out" with their strong coffee in this enticing setting.

Focusing on such emotional passions is also the best way to develop a meaningful expression of the brand personality, because the brand's relationship with the consumer will be much stronger and more motivating when it is based on these feelings. Shelly Lazarus, the current president of Ogilvy & Mather, eloquently described this emotion-based relationship in Pfizer's 2001 annual report:

> Brands are complex. They are created out of main points of contact with the customer. It's not just product functions and features that drive the brand relationship. Rather, it's a myriad of interactions—some commercial and pre-ordained, some ambient and unpredictable … The best companies today understand that it's essential to build a relationship between their brand and their customers—one that takes into consideration every interaction. To do this requires a full understanding of what customers feel about the brand and what they expect.

Good marketing requires ongoing vigilance of these customer wants, as needs are constantly evolving and perceptions change with these market dynamics and the influence of competitive actions. This means maintaining a steady dialog with consumers, usually with qualitative research such as focus groups, one-on-one interviews, or online chat rooms. It is important to add a fresh perspective whenever possible. Marketers who have held the same responsibilities for a long time may not easily notice subtle trends and changes, so adding new marketing talent to participate in research, examining different product categories, and exploring markets abroad can be vital for identifying new ideas. In addition, conducting quantitative tests or tracking studies to capture signs of emerging attitudes and usage habits will help marketers keep their brand marketing fresh and relevant.

There are many dimensions to a consumer need, and it requires astute intuition, an open mind, and various types of creativity to understand the implications of each need. The biggest challenge is to gain a perspective on the relative importance of these different needs, and determine how one can distinguish their brand from the competition and deliver against these top priority needs. Identifying the physical needs is easier, and in some cases may be enough. However, by probing and laddering back on the hierarchy of consumer perceptions, one can gain some unique insights that could help dimensionalize a brand positioning. SnackWell's cookies from Nabisco did a good job of this by combining two different needs in its positioning: the basic snacking indulgence with the emerging desire for dietary health.

Assessing these consumer needs within the context of the overall market trends and opportunities will help a brand positioning seem more innovative and distinct in several ways:

Creating or Extending a Category: Probably the most visible recent example is the erectile dysfunction category. The first entry—Pfizer's Viagra—shaped this segment, but the market potential proved so vast that subsequent entries such as Cialis (Eli Lilly) and Levitra (Bayer/GSK) have been able to carve out significant businesses and extend the category. Similarly, Procter & Gamble's Pampers played the same role as Viagra by creating an entirely new market segment (i.e., the disposable diaper business) years ago.

Gaining Ownership: With clever research and steady advertising support, a brand can develop and then own a dimension of a basic need in a way that establishes an impenetrable niche for a category. P&G marketers heard from consumers that bad breath was most prominent in the morning, so they coined the expression "morning breath" for their Scope Mouthwash advertising (now copyrighted). Another example is Oreo which owns their "signature" dunking the cookie in milk.

Expanding a Target Group: It is important to always be on the lookout for new ways to leverage an established brand need or usage by fine-tuning a positioning, even with a new product, for a peripheral target group. The core of Neutrogena's legacy has always been associated with its translucent amber bar of soap. Johnson & Johnson's research showed that teenagers were familiar with and admired their soap purchased and used by mothers, but they felt it wasn't enough for their acne problems. So Neutrogena introduced a similar product, an amber "Acne-Prone Skin Bar" for teens, which met their needs for gentle cleaning and, more importantly, controlling acne breakout.

Creating a New Use: In the medical business, there is a steady supply of independent research that can occasionally turn up a new opportunity for an established brand. A classic example is Bayer, when clinical studies revealed the benefits of pure aspirin in helping to prevent heart attacks. There is always a risk of diluting your base positioning when touting a completely different benefit, but Bayer's advertising kept its primary use in focus with its selling line, "Powerful Pain Relief ... And So Much More."

Competitive Framework

This answers the question "against whom" from the customer's standpoint. The importance of identifying your main competition cannot be overstated. We are living in a very competitive world, and a brand will never succeed unless it offers a better option in the consumer's mind. By defining the competitive substitutes available for your customer, the marketer can also establish the primary sources of revenue for his/her brand and guide marketing programs accordingly.

In-depth research will be needed to learn all about the competitive brands, primarily from the consumer's perspective, including their perceptions of the benefits, usage (loyalty, frequency, potential limitations, etc.), the brand image or reputation, price/value, product quality, performance, packaging, and all other strengths and weaknesses. Ideally, the positioning must somehow convince the target customer that its brand is indeed different and even superior to the primary competition.

Positioning a brand against the right set of competitors can help create the best potential image. Consumer perceptions are changing all the time, especially with the introduction of new products and re-positioning efforts by competition.

Taking an example from the food industry, consumers' attitudes toward and usage of salty snacks have become far more complex. Around 1990, purchases of salty snacks were based more on expected performance and benefits, such as a sense of indulgence, health (better for you) options, and availability of complements like salsa dip.

These changing market conditions opened the door for new products and line extensions, with a positioning that reflected both product form and taste expectations. Different snack product forms are now available for each expectation, giving manufacturers more options for the competitive frame of reference positioning.

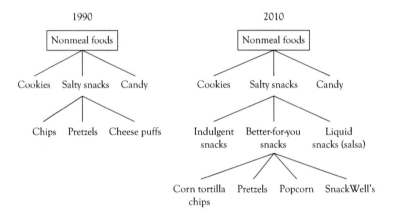

There are other competitive framework considerations for positioning a brand so that its optimal potential is realized. Much depends on a brand's life cycle stage, the relevance and extent of its consumer appeal, and how competitively distinct it is. Some worthwhile positioning tasks include:

Developing a "Specialty" Image: When a brand does not have a major competitive edge and wants to avoid a "me-too" image, it can focus on its primary strength or usage base. Excedrin re-positioned itself to "specialize" in a large volume segment of the pain reliever category, to become "the world's headache medicine of choice."

Separating Yourself from the Crowd: In a very competitive segment such as the pain reliever category, it often makes sense to emphasize a particular point of difference, even if it is not the main benefit of a brand. By focusing on the fact that it does not cause an upset stomach, Tylenol with its acetaminophen formula further differentiated itself from its main competitors Advil, Bayer, and Aleve.

Comparing Yourself to the Category Leader: Brands that want to quickly establish an image of high quality and gain immediate acceptability will refer to a leading brand (often called the "gold standard") when discussing product attributes. Examples of such competitive frameworks include Minute Maid Frozen Orange comparing itself to the real orange flavor and taste of Tropicana's Pure Premium ready-to-serve orange juice, the Pepsi challenge to the world leader, Coca-Cola, and even Honda describing how the all-terrain maneuverability of its new four-wheel Passport SUV is comparable to the ultimate in performance, the Porsche 911.

Expanding the Competitive Framework: When the focused positioning of brands becomes well established, a brand can sometimes enlarge its potential by adapting a broader definition for its competitive framework: Boston Market building on its solid reputation as a fast food chicken restaurant chain to become known more for its "fast food home-cooked meals," and Ensure expanding its niche as a hospital supplement to a line of nutritional, everyday supplements.

How a brand is categorized in relation to its competition also has implications for in-store shelf placement and merchandising. If the perception or net impression of the positioning is rather special or proprietary compared with its main competitor, then the product should be placed next to this other product. If the brand is strong and can claim a broader range of competition, then there may be additional point-of-purchase placements at retail that could expand trial. For example, referring to Oreo as a sweet snack and not just a chocolate-based cookie may encourage retailers to stock Oreo in more than one section of the store.

Benefit or Promise

This should describe the single, most meaningful promise that can be offered to the prime prospect, which would make it seem special and different from the identified competition. The benefit should answer the basic question, "what's in it for me?" It is not what the product does, but what it does _for_ the consumer—how it resolves his/her problem and ideally makes the consumer feel. The benefit is really a promise of something that adds value and addresses a relevant need or desire of the target customer. Only the consumer can really answer these questions of relevance, including whether the benefit should be positioned as a functional or emotional one.

This third element of the positioning statement—benefits—follows (1) the target customer and needs and (2) the competitive framework simply because the first two elements generally define the optimal benefit for a brand. Success will be attained only if a benefit can effectively address a particular need or desire of the primary target customer in a way that seems different from the competition. This is not an easy task, however. It will require a great deal of smart research and creativity to determine exactly how the benefit can be truly meaningful, appealing, and different. Some critical considerations for this analysis are outlined below.

Types of Needs/Benefits: Earlier we discussed physical and emotional needs. Understanding the nature of these needs, especially how compelling and special they are, will help you define the desired benefit at different sequential levels:

- _Product Benefits:_ Simply identifying the main functions or what a product or service does vis-à-vis the basic physical or functional needs. For example, Tide Detergent cleans clothes, gets out dirt, and removes stains.
- _Customer Benefits:_ Looking at the implications of this function from the customer perspective, what it means to the customer, or what it does for him/her. In the case of Tide, it keeps clothes cleaner longer, they're softer and more comfortable, and they need fewer washes.
- _Emotional Benefits:_ Usually this represents the most compelling reason for choosing a brand, the way to the customer's heart. It's all about feelings. This is a benefit of the highest order and will most likely be the best building block for that trusting relationship between the brand and the customer. Using Tide as an example again, the emotional "pay-off" or

benefit is the feeling of pride in your clean clothes, how this will reflect on you and members of your family, plus the basic confidence of making a good impression.

Identifying the emotional "hot button" and being able to articulate it in a meaningful consumer language is probably the biggest challenge for marketers. Branding is about perceptions, so research should focus on how consumers construe their own problems and views, what insights can be picked up and then tested with further research, and finally expressing a dimension of the benefit that will strike this emotional chord with the target customer.

In problem-oriented categories such as the pharmaceutical business, the desired feeling one can experience on solving the problem is often the ultimate "clincher" for trying a product. Marketing for the prescription brand Fosamax, for example, focused on the inherent fear of osteoporosis with the theme "Fight Your Fear." Print ads had headlines like "Since I found out about my osteoporosis, I've been afraid to walk to my mailbox when it rains." The copy explained how Fosamax rebuilds bone and bone strength (product benefit) so the consumer can do what he/she wants (customer benefit) and, most importantly, restores his/her confidence that will help overcome this fear (emotional benefit).

One should not ignore the potential of a customer benefit when a new product can offer a real breakthrough advantage, however. When Polaroid was first introduced, its instant development process was so revolutionary that emphasis on anything but this product benefit detracted from the key selling point and point of difference.

EffectiveBrands, a global marketing consultancy, extends these types of benefits to include "purposeful benefits," especially for big global brands. At the bottom of the benefit ladder is "functional benefits." HTC is an example of a brand that promises fast download speeds, but no emotional benefit, and hence it is difficult to relate to the HTC brand as a person. Stella Artois leverages its 600-year-old heritage to interact with consumers on the best ways to pour and drink its beer, which creates a credible relationship and an emotional, trustful experience.

At the top of the benefit ladder is "purposeful benefits," which offer a societal purpose even beyond a firm's "corporate social responsibility." This type of benefit should relate to the essence of the brand and leverage its integrity to make the world a better place. Examples of brands that offer such a purposeful benefit are:

- **Dove:** Stands for real beauty
- **The Body Shop:** Against animal cruelty
- **FedEx:** Sustainability connecting people and places

Consistent with this view of "purposeful benefits," Marc Pritchard, the Global Marketing and Brand Building Officer at P&G, at a recent world conference talked about building brands to serve a higher purpose that will in turn produce more sustainable business results. Marc commented that "we must change from marketing to consumers to serving our consumers." He added that today's consumers are asking for more from brands, "they want to help the world, not just themselves, and as a result will choose those brands that share their value beliefs."

Competitive Benchmarking: The perception of a brand is often shaped by how it stacks up against a familiar competitor, so selecting the rival brand for this comparison can be crucial. There is a natural tendency for manufacturers to immediately stereotype or categorize a brand, typically as a result of a market segmentation analysis. The retailer will think this way too, because his mind focuses on product sections of a store. But the consumer will invariably view a brand's position, or at least their expectations for its performance, in a different light.

A few years ago, my company did some research in the United States for a new dessert wine from southern Spain. These wines were certainly drunk and perceived as very popular dessert wines in Spain, but dessert wine drinkers in the United States, to our surprise, did not view this Spanish product as a dessert wine at all, as it was much darker, heavier, with higher alcohol levels compared with other dessert wines in America. With further research we realized that the profile of the best potential target user should instead be those who drank liqueurs, not dessert wines per se. The product's final positioning was as a "wine liqueur," a conclusion reached only by re-defining the target audience profile and hence the competitive framework for this re-positioned brand.

A useful analytical tool to diagnose these perceptions and expectations versus competition is the Brand Asset Profile. After fully researching a given category and identifying the underlying customer needs and main competitors recognized by the customer, research determines the most important, prevalent perceptions of the strengths and vulnerabilities for your brand versus the competition. The objective is to select and leverage the perceived strength that would be most compelling for positioning a brand, which should ideally address a burning customer need and capitalize on the perceived vulnerability of the brand's main competitor.

Single or Multiple Benefits? This is a very complex issue for many manufacturers. From a strategic and communication standpoint, the greater the focus, the more successful you will be in conveying a message, distinguishing yourself from the competition, and establishing an image of a "specialty" product. But this raises other practical and business questions. Are the expectations too high and can you deliver on a single-minded promise that implies "the best?" Is the business potential sufficient to justify such a narrow focus? Do you offer a benefit that you "own" and cannot be duplicated easily by the competition?

Excedrin took this route when it positioned itself as "The Headache Medicine." The highly saturated, mature analgesics category was an environment where a niche-oriented positioning made the most practical sense for Excedrin. By reaching out primarily to consumers with severe headaches, implicitly the kind that could not be relieved as effectively by competition, Excedrin created a specialty image among these sufferers as the strongest, most powerful remedy for this problem.

Positioning an "umbrella brand" that is powerful and offers more than one benefit can give the consumer the impression of added value, that he/she will be getting more for their money. Successful brands can introduce line extensions that address multiple needs, especially when the related benefits are perceived as an extension of the core strength of the brand. Tylenol PM is positioned as a combination of an analgesic and a sleep aid. This appeals to the same basic target group, because users view a good night's sleep as another way to help relieve their pain. Tylenol can get away with this multiple benefit strategy because of its strong position in the market and ample budgets to communicate these related benefits.

Some brands have been developed on a multiple benefit platform mainly because of their traditional usage and the attitudes of consumers. Perhaps, the best example is Arm & Hammer Baking Soda from Church & Dwight, where I spent time as head of New Products. This was a sleepy brand, yet was used in almost every household in the United States for over a century. In the early 1970s, however, focus groups revealed that many housewives put it in their refrigerator to absorb odors. This led to a new positioning, backed by new advertising, and sales exploded. More research showed how Arm & Hammer had long been considered the ultimate multiuse product, with housewives using it for everything from poison ivy relief and bathing to putting out fires and cleaning teeth.

After advertising its new positioning for absorbing odors in refrigerators, Church & Dwight started developing a wide array of different products under the Arm & Hammer brand name, stretching itself to such diverse and unrelated uses that the trust for the Arm & Hammer brand showed signs of being undermined. We re-grouped and asked ourselves how far this brand could be stretched before jeopardizing its inherent integrity. By re-examining all these uses and looking for common themes, we concluded that the usage of Arm & Hammer Baking Soda, as an ingredient in line extensions or re-positioned uses of the base product, had a higher chance of success if it remained in the categories of cleaning and deodorizing. Fortunately, these two basic usage categories were very diverse and provided ample opportunities for a steady stream of new products for years to come.

Features and Benefits: While this comparison is certainly not new, the exercise can be very helpful in encouraging people to take a step beyond the obvious functional aspects of a product or service, and answer the question of what it actually does *for* the customer. Such features are facts, or generally refer to the attributes of a product. They can be important if they relate to how to satisfy a customer need, and are more appropriate for convincing someone that the promise or benefit is indeed credible (i.e., part of the "reasons why" in the positioning statement).

Benefits are about the significance of these features, or how it adds value or offers some kind of "gain" for the customer. As such, they must be deemed highly relevant for the target customer, ideally with an emotional element. As an example, a toothpaste may have special ingredients that contain bleach and whiten your teeth (feature and its function), but importantly it makes the customer *feel* more attractive (the emotional benefit).

Ideally, the benefit should be a selling idea that is distinct, or at least perceived to be different from the competition, although this is becoming increasingly difficult in reality. This is why more companies are focusing on the ultimate brand personality, together with a well-positioned benefit and support, to create a net impression of being special and standing out. Good research and experienced analysis will often reveal new consumer insights that become the basis for a novel or different benefit. Some key questions or criteria for identifying an optimal benefit for a brand positioning include the following:

1. Can the benefit be modified for different target segments of the audience?
2. How meaningful, compelling, or important is the benefit?
3. Is it truly unique, or at least perceived this way, compared to the competition or the category?
4. Does the benefit fit a market "gap" or address a certain consumer dissatisfaction in a competitive area?
5. Is the benefit proprietary, patentable, ownable, or preemptive? Can the competition copy it?
6. What is most relevant and would generate the most interest, the functional or emotional benefit?
7. Are there other secondary benefits worth identifying, or will this dilute the impact of being single minded and focused?
8. Can you satisfactorily deliver on the promised benefit and adequately meet the customer's expectations?

Over time, successful brands have reinforced a single-minded benefit repeatedly to a point where today they practically own a particular promise. Here are some examples of brands that are immediately associated with a specific benefit, to the extent that they "own" it:

Brand	Category	"Owned benefit"
Volvo	Cars	Safety
Domino's Pizza	Pizza/fast food	Delivery
Wal-Mart	Retail	Low prices
Southwest Airlines	Airlines	Low prices
FedEx	Shipping	Overnight delivery
Dell	Computers	Buy direct
Maytag	Appliances	Reliability
Coke	Beverages	Original/heritage
Pepsi	Beverages	Younger generation
Listerine	Mouthwash	Kills germs
Lysol	Cleaning/bathroom	Kills germs
Crest	Toothpaste	Fights cavities
Colgate	Toothpaste	Whitening
Aquafresh	Toothpaste	Tartar control
Close-Up	Toothpaste	Fresher breath

Reasons Why (or Reasons to Believe)

These are often the most important factors for differentiating and selecting a particular brand. These support points basically legitimize the benefit, make the promise credible, and help to clarify how it is different from competition. Marketers frequently refer to this as the "Reason to Believe" (RTB).

While the benefit should focus on what a product does for the consumer, the reality is that the desired impression for most consumer products does not vary significantly. Most deal with some dimension of product quality or customer satisfaction, and so it is a real challenge to define a benefit that is entirely unique in itself. What is needed to make a brand appear distinctive and ideally proprietary is the combination of the benefit and relevant support. The specific "reasons why" or "permission-to-believe" points will depend on the consumer needs and the nature of the benefit, and generally fall into four types:

Logical Explanation: This is anything that helps explain how a product works or solves a problem, especially if it is a proprietary process. For example, Fosamax refers to how it builds bones and gets you moving again to help you fight osteoporosis and its debilitating effects.

Hard Evidence: A common rationale used for OTC brands involves the special design features or ingredients in the formulation as proof of performance. Often, the favorable results are communicated in the form of a picture or graphic illustration. For example, Coors Beer claims it is the only beer made with "Rocky Mountain Spring Water," which makes it more refreshing.

Outside Recommendations: Any kind of endorsement from a professional organization, independent study, or even a celebrity spokesman can help build credibility for the basic promises. Tylenol's proprietary claim of "hospital recommended" has become a classic. Michael Jordan is still one of the most respected spokesmen, and he was a key reason for Nike's success.

Brand Track Record and Heritage: Reference to a brand's origin and/or proven success in the past can be a compelling RTB in a brand's promise. Michelin tires have a strong reputation for high quality, reinforced by a very emotional visual—a baby in a tire slot—and the tagline reminder, "because so much is riding on your tires." This "reason why" has established Michelin as the brand of choice for anxious, safety-conscious parents of young children. Other brands refer to their source to leverage memorable images associated with a specific place: Evian from the Alps, Godiva from Belgium, and Jack Daniels from the Tennessee Mountains. Many countries have developed a reputation of strength in certain product areas, and some companies have effectively leveraged this heritage:

- Japan: electronics (Sony) and automobiles (Sony, Nissan, Honda, Toyota, and Mitsubishi)
- Germany: cars (BMW, Mercedes-Benz, Audi, VW)
- France: perfumes (Chanel), wines, and fashion clothes

- ○ Ireland: crystal (Waterford) and linen
- ○ England: china (Wedgwood), wool
- ○ Switzerland: watches, cheese, banking services
- ○ Italy: leather, shoes, pasta, wine
- ○ Russia: vodka, fur
- ○ Middle East: carpets, oil
- ○ Mexico: silver, crafts, beer (Corona)
- ○ Colombia: coffee
- ○ Australia: eggs, wool

Focus and simplicity are critical for making a long-lasting, positive impression in consumers' minds. All too often, the product-oriented mentality is preoccupied with so many novel features of a product, and is insistent on listing all these attributes as the "reasons why." This desire must be controlled, because a brand positioning is stronger when it is single minded and succinct. Sometimes related product features can be integrated and communicated using one analogous benchmark. For example, Reach toothbrush had several distinctive features that supported the benefit of cavity prevention—angled neck, higher and lower bristles, and compact head. J&J wrapped up these subselling points with the encompassing expression "like a dental instrument," a simple notion that made its positioning for cavity prevention even more powerful.

Another way to reinforce a brand's benefit/promise is through co-branding. However, this will only work when the other brand shares the same type and level of perceived quality, and there is no risk of brand dilution or sales erosion of each business. Häagen-Dazs is well known for its super-premium ice cream, but the brand is all about the emotional experience: "provides personal, unadulterated pleasure, which starts in the mind (anticipation), travels through the mouth and ends up in the mind (satisfaction)." To further dimensionalize the brand and add interest in their frozen novelties, Häagen-Dazs teamed up with Pepperidge Farm to offer super-premium ice cream sandwiches. This co-branding effort leveraged the strong reputation for premium quality of two non-conflicting brands to create a synergistic, competitively unique brand proposition.

The Brand Essence—Its "Personality"

The personality or character of a brand is a manifestation of the positioning. Whereas the positioning is stated in business or strategic terminology, the brand personality enriches the positioning and gives it a life. It uses adjectives and analogies that make it sound more like a person or a memorable experience.

The brand character describes who the brand is as a personage. The brand should not be described as a "thing"—product, service, or organization. Instead, using language that describes the relevant personality traits will enable you to create an image or brand identity that generates an impression that is much easier for consumers to relate to, feel comfortable with, and remember in a positive light.

A positioning is not the same as a brand. Positioning provides more details on how to rationally describe a product or service in terms of the target customer needs, the physical attributes or "reasons why," and the differences from competition. The brand personality captures the essence or inner soul of what a brand should mean to consumers on an emotional or nonrational level. This brand essence transcends the physical attributes of the product/service and does not reference competition (neither the "best" nor "better than"). Importantly, this inner brand personality or "DNA" of the brand endures over time, never changing, even when marketed in foreign cultures. It is the constant face of the brand to the consumer.

Conversely, other elements of the positioning may be adjusted to address changes in the marketplace—competitive threats, emerging consumer habits, new innovations, and different target audience segments and their needs and cultural values. However, any modifications to the positioning should be rare and kept to a minimum, and never alter the brand essence. Here are some examples:

Kraft's Philadelphia Cream Cheese

Brand Essence: "My daily trip to paradise"
Positioning: "For consumers with full, busy lives, Philadelphia is the brand of cream cheese that provides a little reward every day because of its unique indulgent taste and texture"

Coca-Cola

Brand Essence: "Refreshes the mind, body and spirit"

Positioning: "For consumers looking for refreshment, Coke is the brand of refreshment beverage that provides a lift to the body and spirit because of its unique taste, carbonation, and conviviality"

The contrast of brand image between Coke and Pepsi shows how two very similar beverages make a very different impression. Coke, the market leader, uses a classic number one brand strategy. It is representative of a category leadership philosophy—steady, consistent, almost stodgy with no risk-taking moves, and always conservative—making only slight refinements (except for its blunder with "Classic Coke") to ensure that it keeps this position. Coke's brand image and ad campaigns are filled with "Americana" associations such as baseball and apple pie.

Pepsi crafted its brand personality to strike a marked difference from Coke. As the number two cola brand, it is much more pioneering, risk-taking, innovative, and vivacious—reminiscent of the famous Avis "We try Harder" campaign against the category leader, Hertz. Pepsi took aim directly at the heaviest soft drink user segment, the youth of America. With personality traits that include "fun, active, and adventuresome," it created the memorable "Pepsi Generation" campaign. Pepsi's proprietary brand personality offers such a strong emotional and contagious appeal that it is not only endeared by today's youth but also embraced by all who think and feel young.

Here are some other examples of the "brand essence" for famous brands:

- Nike   Bringing inspiration to every athlete
- Starbucks   Rewarding every day moments
- Hallmark   Cared sharing
- Disney   Fun family entertainment
- Nature Conservancy   Saving great places
- McDonald's   Fast foods served with home values
- Anheuser-Busch   Adding to life's enjoyment
- UPS   We enable global commerce
- Microsoft Windows   Advancing everyday accomplishments

- ESPN   There is no such thing as too much sports
- Accenture   Innovation delivered
- AT&T   Your world delivered
- Malibu Rum   Exotic easy-going fun
- Visit Scotland   The natural wonder of northern Europe
- Mercedes-Benz   Engineering excellence
- BMW   Driving excellence
- Pepsi   Youthful independence
- Suave   Smart beauty
- Dove   Real beauty
- Pyrex   Inspiring confidence in the kitchen

Using Analogies to Help Define Brands

The specific description for this succinct brand essence is not always easy to develop. The brand personality evolves from a great deal of research on the customer, the competition, and the market, so it is natural to have divergent views on what this inner brand soul should consist of. A common tactic is to use analogies that will help characterize a brand. Familiar benchmarks such as celebrities, animals, cars, and magazines can help dimensionalize a brand, stimulating new insights on various personality traits. These benchmarks will also ultimately help to communicate the full personality make-up to the creative people and other outside suppliers who must execute this brand positioning with new advertising, packaging design, public relations, promotions, and so on.

As a first step, select some of the more obvious personality traits that you think would fit the positioning. Then start thinking of different analogies. You can pick a famous person like Harrison Ford, Winston Churchill, Britney Spears, or Barack Obama who have the same traits and values as the brand. Or take a well-defined profession, such as a doctor, policeman, athlete, or scientist, which has a certain stereotyped image that reflects the character of a brand. Maybe an animal like an elephant, tiger, mouse, or gorilla would be a better fit. You could take this line of analogous thinking one step further by imagining what this person would wear and talk about at a party. This thought process opens the mind and helps crystallize the imagined personality of a brand.

The use of analogous benchmarks with recognizable personalities or images can be very effective when it describes a noteworthy contrast, especially when comparing a brand to another competitor. For example:

- David Bowie versus Pavarotti
- Meryl Streep versus Madonna
- Tom Hanks versus Hulk Hogan
- A lion versus a pussycat
- A duck versus an eagle
- A paper cup versus a crystal goblet

Other Ways to Distinguish a Brand Personality

A common challenge is to describe a brand personality in very basic terms, ideally using the language of average people, plus plenty of examples, to minimize any misunderstanding by outside creative functions and even internal ones such as sales people. These descriptors should be more unique to articulate your personality and to bring a brand to life, and <u>not</u> overuse words like "trust" or "leader." For example:

- **Using One Word:** For example, "Irreverent" for Doritos brand, later used for its line extension "Cool Ranch." Other examples of brands with a single-word focus that helps to visualize their band personality include:
    o Volvo—safety
    o BMW—sporty
    o Mercedes—prestige
    o Heinz (ketchup)—thick
    o FedEx—overnight
- **Comparison:** A defining adjective to favorably juxtapose its brand personality to a competitor:
    o Virgin Airlines being "cheeky" (impudent, yet fun) versus British Airways being "smug"
    o An Apple Mac being casual, cool, and self-assured versus the PC character as stuffy, overly-anxious, and fidgety (very well communicated in Apple's "I'm a Mac" TV ad campaign— see http://www.youtube.com/watch?v=C5z0Ia5jDt4)

I'm a PC   I'm a Mac

- **Expression of Feeling:** Like the "thought bubble" in comics, describing how you want your user to feel about the brand as a person. For example, to describe **Charles Schwab**— "Here's a straight shooter, someone who never has hidden agendas or ulterior motives—the only one not requiring a poker face…"
- **When at a Party:** Describe what music/drinks would be appropriate when your brand shows up at a party. For example (often used in focus groups):
  - Wal-Mart—country western, mixed with patriotic songs for a "down-home" block partier, drinking Busch beer
  - Target—as the "whatever" convivial partier, alternative music, drinking cherry kamikazes
- **Fit in Another Category:** Identifying the optimal "home" for a brand. For example, which retailer would be the best fit for a particular special skin care brand (a method often used in research):
  - Abercrombie & Fitch
  - Banana Republic
  - The Gap
  - Hugo Boss
  - Talbot's

Common Problems and Challenges With Today's Brands

The pursuit of "brand distinctiveness" is never easy. So many brand marketers tend to use words that are over used or just too general. Smart research and creativity are critical for going beyond the norm and selecting terms that are more specific and vibrant. For example, some common, vague emotional descriptors include: "trust," "peace of mind," "dependable," "empowerment," and "caring."

The reality is that such brand personality descriptors represent only the threshold for many categories, often called "cost-of-entry" terminology. Brands competing in certain categories must at least convey an impression that active consumers expect at a minimum:

- Pharmaceuticals   "Trust"
- Telecommunications   "Empowerment"
- Whiskey   "Status"
- Cleaning   "Caring"

Other common mistakes include inadequate research that doesn't go in-depth to probe the minds and hearts of consumers, not including any key emotions in the positioning statement or strategy, or simply making promises that represent wishful thinking, with no chance of delivering. Instead, marketers have to be disciplined to go beyond these common "directional emotions" when articulating a brand personality profile, to reflect varying levels of the emotional intensity, to use basic consumer language, and to create multi-dimensional touch points so that emotional connections at least reach the subconscious part of the brain. Only by applying smart research and creativity can the marketer differentiate the brand more clearly from competition and develop proprietary, memorable expressions and analogies.

Brand Archetypes

In their 1999 book *The Hero and the Outlaw: Building Extraordinary Brands Through the Power of Archetypes*, Margaret Mark and Carol Pearson define a variety of stereotypes to aid this brand description task:

The Innocent:

- Wholesome, pure
- Forgiving, trusting, honest
- Happy, optimistic, enjoy simple pleasures

The Explorer (or "Seeker"):

- Searcher, seeker, adventurous, restless, desire excitement
- Independent, self-directed, self-sufficient
- Value freedom

The Sage:

- Thinker, philosopher, reflective
- Expert, advisor, teacher
- Confident, in-control, self-contained, credible

The Hero (or "Warrior"):

- Warrior, competitive, aggressive, winner
- Principled, idealist, challenges "wrongs," improves the world
- Proud, brave, courageous, sacrifices for greater good

The Outlaw (or "Destroyer"):

- Rebellious, shocking, outrageous, disruptive
- Fearful, powerful
- Counter cultural, revolutionary, liberated

The Magician:

- Shaman, healer, spiritual, holistic, intuitive
- Values magical moments and special rituals
- Catalyst for change, charismatic

The Regular Guy/Gal (or "Orphan"):

- Not pretentious, straight shooter, people oriented
- Reliable, dependable, practical, down to earth
- Values routines, predictability, the status quo, traditional

The Lover:

- Seeks true love, intimacy, sensuality
- Passionate, sexy, seductive, erotic
- Sees pleasure to indulge, follows emotions

The Jester:

- Clown, jester, trickster
- Playful, takes things lightly, creates a little fun/chaos
- Impulsive, spontaneous, lives in the moment

The Caregiver:

- Altruistic, selfless
- Nurturing, compassionate, empathetic
- Supportive, generous

The Creator:

- Innovative, imaginative, artistic
- Experimental, willing to take risks
- Ambitious, desire to turn ideas into reality

The Ruler:

- Manager, organizer, takes charge attitude
- Efficient, productive
- Confident, responsible, role model

These prototypes are admittedly subjective, but they do help by categorizing various personality traits with a descriptive label. The authors, Mark and Pearson, mention several celebrities, companies, and product brands that share qualities of these archetypes. In addition, when discussing these archetypes in my NYU branding course, I always ask the students to think of actual people or brands that may fit some of these stereotypes. Here are some noteworthy examples, from my students and the book, that can further dimensionalize these descriptions and "add some flesh to the bone":

- **The Innocent:** Doris Day, Tom Hanks, Forest Gump, Shirley Temple, Disney, Breyers Ice Cream, Ronald McDonald, Baskin Robbins
- **The Explorer:** Huckleberry Finn, Anita Roddick (founder—The Body Shop), Charles Lindberg, Earnest Shackleton, Jeep, Starbucks
- **The Sage:** Oprah Winfrey, Walter Cronkite, Gandolph (Lord of the Rings), CNN, NPR, Intel, HP, *NY Times*, MIT, Harvard, Mayo Clinic
- **The Hero:** John Wayne, John Glenn, JFK, MLK, Nelson Mandela, Colin Powell, *Braveheart* (with Mel Gibson), Nike, FedEx, Red Cross, Olympics
- **The Outlaw:** Robin Hood, John Lennon, James Dean, Howard Stern, Jack Nicholson, Maria Calles, Muhammad Ali, Harley Davidson, Apple, MTV
- **The Magician:** Harry Potter, Yoda (*Star Wars*), Mary Poppins, Dannon Yogurt, MasterCard (priceless ad campaign), Weight Watchers
- **Regular Guy/Girl:** Cal Ripken, Woody Guthrie, *Hoosiers* (movie), Ben & Jerry's, Saturn (car), Avis, Visa
- **The Lover:** Clark Gable, Cary Grant, Elizabeth Taylor, Sophia Loren, Cinderella, Casablanca, Revlon, Victoria's Secret, Godiva
- **The Jester:** Charlie Chaplin, Steve Martin, Mae West, Jay Leno, Marx Brothers, M&M's, Snickers
- **The Caregiver:** Princess Diana, Florence Nightingale, Mother Teresa, Bob Hope, Campbell's Soup, GE, Coca-Cola, James Stewart in *Wonderful Life*
- **The Creator:** Pablo Picasso, Georgia O'Keeffe, Martha Stewart, Crayola, Sherwin-Williams, William Sonoma, Sesame Street
- **The Ruler:** Ralph Lauren, Microsoft, American Express, CitiBank, IRS, The White House, Cadillac

The authors explain these archetypes using historical myths, analogies, and beliefs, supplemented by examples of current brands throughout their book. Market researchers often refer to these archetypes when analyzing perceptions by consumers of different brands. For example, if the findings indicate that the archetypes for two close competitors are the same, it raises a "red flag" that the client's brand image should be modified to appear more distinct.

Marketers find such archetypes helpful when defining their brand personality. Such detailed archetype descriptions create a sharper image for all communications initiatives. Using such prototypes can go a long way to charge up the creative juices and to apply this personification to all strategic positioning elements in a way that relates to the inherent desires of the primary target user. Here are some corporate brand images reflecting these archetypes:

1. Coca-Cola—The Innocent
2. Microsoft—The Ruler
3. IBM—The Sage, with a Jester component (from the old advertising campaign with Charlie Chaplin)
4. GE—The Caregiver (or Ruler)
5. Nokia—The Explorer
6. Intel—The Sage
7. Disney—The Innocent
8. Ford—The Hero (trucks/cars) and Explorer (SUVs)
9. McDonald's—The Innocent
10. AT&T—The Caregiver
11. Marlboro—The Creator
12. Mercedes—The Ruler

The End Result: The Full Positioning Statement

The final positioning statement may be deceptively simple, yet the research and analysis that shape this summary can be exhaustive. But it is all worth it. The brand positioning is the heart of all marketing. It is the main tool for developing and then judging all brand communications, whether it involves advertising, personal selling, or a simple business card. Here is an example of one of the largest consumer brands, P&G's Tide, the leader in detergents:

> **For Target Consumer and Needs:** Moms with active children and husbands … who have heavy-duty cleaning needs and want to keep their clothes and their families looking their best
> **Brand:** Tide is the brand of choice among…
> **Competitive Framework:** … laundry care detergent products, that …

Benefit: … is best for your clothes (cleaning, protecting fabrics, etc.) and you, because …

Reason Why: … (a) it has a special formulation with heavy-duty cleaners (e.g., grease-releasers), special fabric protectors (e.g., color guard), and (b) it is endorsed by authoritative sources

Brand Personality: Tide is strong (like a rock), traditional, dependable, commanding, yet practical

The Brand Pyramid

Another positioning tool is the brand pyramid, developed by Larry Light at BBDO several years ago. This is particularly useful for focusing on the emotional benefits and the brand personality. It defines the essence of the brand by connecting the rational position to the emotional framework. It starts at the bottom by identifying the product features, then moves up to highlight the functional and emotional benefits, then the user values, and finally brand personality at the peak. Here is how this positioning tool is used to define the Wrangler brand (in the United Kingdom):

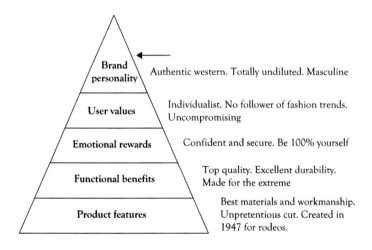

Other Brand Positioning Statement Formats

Many companies use positioning statements that closely resemble the basic format described in this book, but with slightly different or additional elements. For example, Nabisco includes an important aspect that is critical for its extremely competitive categories, "A Leverageable Point of Difference," which identifies a specific feature that distinguishes its brand from the competition. This point of difference for Oreo's positioning is its "superbly delicious taste and fun eating ritual." Unilever adds even more components to its positioning format—for example, insights, values & personality, and discriminators—as shown in the figure below.

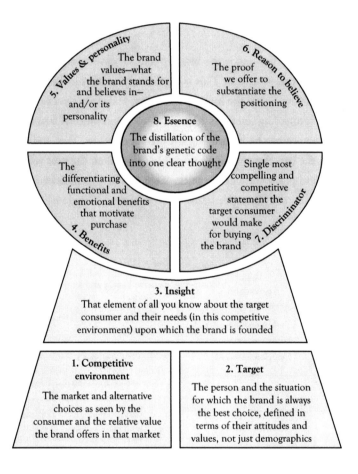

A Strategic Challenge: How to Make a Positioning Seem Different?

With the advancement of performance capabilities for so many products, plus the stricter regulations on claims, it has become difficult to create a brand impression that is truly distinct. This basically involves transitioning from getting the big or "right" idea to getting the idea right. This is a strategic challenge. Here are some common strategies that have effectively differentiated well-known brands when the actual differences are minimal:

1. **Leadership Position:** This is perhaps the most powerful way to distinguish a brand, supplemented by its sales, technology, or performance credentials. For example:
   a. Heinz owns ketchup
   b. Xerox as the original copier
   c. Hershey's as the chocolate leader
   d. Campbell's dominates soups
2. **Heritage:** Highlighting the unique history of a brand will make people feel more secure in their choice, for a brand that is more emotionally trusted. For example:
   a. **Steinway:** "The instrument of the immortals"
   b. **Cross Pens:** "Flawless classics since 1846"
   c. **Coca-Cola:** The "original"
3. **Specialist:** Creating a perception of an "expert" in a particular category (usually retail) or activity—for example, retailers like The Limited, Victoria's Secret, Crate & Barrel, and Banana Republic.
4. **Endorsement:** People often want some kind of affirmation of their selection, called "preference positioning," which indicates their tendency to want to "join the bandwagon" for greater confidence. Examples include:
   a. **Tylenol:** The pain reliever hospitals prefer
   b. **Nike:** The choice of famous athletes like Michael Jordan and Tiger Woods
   c. **Lexus:** Highest ratings on customer satisfaction (J.D. Power)
5. **Pricing:** Extremely low- or high-end price points can become a meaningful differentiator. Wal-Mart and Southwest Airlines at the low end, and Häagen-Dazs Ice Cream at the premium end.
6. **Distribution:** A distinctive channel of distribution can be another way to separate a brand from the crowd. For example:

    a. **Avon:** As the primary door-to-door brand

    b. **L'eggs Pantyhose:** Sold using unique display stands in various retail outlets

    c. **Timex:** As the first watch available extensively in drug stores

    d. **Dell:** Selling computers directly online

The Emotional Side of Branding

People with successful relationships have developed over time a strong bond built on shared values and emotions that keeps them together. So it is with brands. Marketers must think of a brand as a person who could provide a relevant, satisfying experience. Ultimately, it is this emotional bonding that will lead to solid brand loyalty and the optimum—strong brand equity.

In theory, one should examine the marketplace to identify new opportunities that will then drive the product development process. The reality in business, however, is that most companies are either developing new products concurrent with this review of the market or start with a new product innovation and then seek a home for it in the market. This approach naturally makes one focus on the specific product attributes and how they may be useful for the consumer.

The big challenge for marketers is to remove themselves from this "manufacturer" mentality and put themselves in the shoes of the customer. This is not always easy. Imagine a brand manager, after extensive research with consumers, telling a brilliant scientist in R&D that their latest creation or advancement is not perceived as relevant or appealing to the customer. Or maybe a completely new way of describing this new product is the only way to generate any enthusiasm and interest by the consumer.

The relatively simple task is to explain what such product advances may do for the consumer. The more difficult part is to convince the consumer that he/she will actually <u>feel</u> a lot different once they use it. Yet getting consumers emotionally attached to a brand is what it will usually take to be a success in the marketplace.

In research, it is important to look for natural emotional reactions to a concept, advertising, or package, as these will usually be more revealing and truthful for any kind of emotional assessment. For example:

Emotions and Behavior

Discoveries in the field of neuroscience have had a major impact on branding in recent years. It started in 1943 with Dr. Maslov's famous paper on the "Theory of Human Motivations," in which he concludes that pure emotions fulfill the ultimate need for "self-actualization":

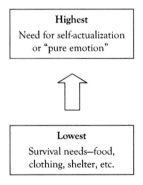

This revelation was followed by other conclusions from noteworthy neuroscientists on how emotions, not cognitive thinking, have the greatest influence on behavior and decision making. And marketing is essentially all about changing people's behavior and convincing them to make a purchase decision. Here are some quotes that confirm the importance of emotions, for example:

> The essential difference between emotion and reason is that emotion leads to action while reason leads to conclusions.
>
> John Caine (2000)

> The wiring of the brain favors emotion—the communications from the emotional to the rational are stronger than the other way around.
>
> Joseph LaDoux (1996)

> Over 80% of thought, emotions and learning occurs in the unconscious mind.
>
> Professor Demasio (1999)

Much of Demasio's thinking was based on a theory by Paul MacLean in the 1960s on the Triune Brain model, which explains how the human brain has evolved. Essentially, this theory explains that we don't have one brain, but three. These are all layered on top of each other and were developed during different stages of evolution:

1. **The Old Brain (Reptilian):** Controls survival behavior and autonomous functions such as heart beats, digestion, movement, and breathing.
2. **The Midbrain:** Known as the limbic system, this is the primary seat for emotions, memories, and attention (i.e., the unconscious).
3. **The New Brain:** This is the neocortex, the logical part of the brain that involves rational thoughts, thinking skills, language, and speech processing.

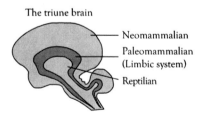

The triune brain

Neomammalian
Paleomammalian (Limbic system)
Reptilian

According to this theory, we are only fully conscious of our new brain, the neocortex. By contrast, the unconscious or midbrain helps you determine what you should pay attention to with your conscious brain. This means that our decision-making behavior is greatly influenced by this unconscious brain. And it is incredibly efficient. Neuroscientists have estimated that our five senses receive 11 million pieces of information every second, with our conscious brain only processing around 40 pieces.

This theory, however accurate the amount of information absorbed, at least underscores the importance of including emotional benefits in a brand positioning, as well as all the touch points when marketing that brand. In the area of graphic design, there is a standard guideline on what communication elements have the most impact on this subconscious part of the brain—the "communications hierarchy."

This communication hierarchy is particularly helpful when developing all the execution aspects of marketing to visually communicate a brand's positioning and personality (e.g., logos, packaging, advertising, websites, brochures).

Seeking Consumer Insights

In this fiercely competitive world, marketers are digging deeper into consumer minds to identify worthwhile voids or issues that will help them leverage their brands. What they are looking for is a distinct or new "consumer insight," usually a problem or challenge that the consumer is not even initially aware of. Such insights are revealed only after dogged prodding in research by experienced, intuitive marketers. Research must focus on the problems or wishes of heavy users in a given category, to try to uncover feelings that are not readily apparent to anyone.

A consumer insight can be defined as a deeply held belief or behavioral pattern that relates to the most important problems or needs in a category—the "hidden" or real hopes of people who use a particular product or service. Most consumer insights are expressed in three different ways:

- As a weakness or shortcoming of competition
- As an obstacle that consumers identify for <u>not</u> using your brand
- A compelling belief or opinion about a category that is not yet recognized.

Discovering relevant consumer insights requires imagination, interpretation, and intuition. You must keep an open mind to be able to "read between the lines" during customer research. Because these underlying attitudes are not obvious, it also takes constant probing. And most importantly, one should recognize that consumer perceptions or opinions are usually more revealing and important than what <u>you</u> think is true.

The Process for Identifying Consumer Insights

1. **Available Research:** Start by re-examining all current data—your "Brand Knowledge" book, supplemental information from the internet—collect data from syndicated sources, and review all past qualitative and quantitative in-house research.
2. **New Perspective:** Take a fresh view and focus on the heavy users in the category, starting with a review of the demographics and psychographics. Then generate as many hypotheses as possible on new or unfulfilled needs, beliefs, or behaviors to create potential concept ideas.
3. **Explore in Research:** Get topline reactions to the most promising concepts in qualitative research (e.g., focus groups, one-on-one interviews, ethnography, or on-site observations), to get some sense of relative interest. Most important, use these concepts to stimulate extensive discussion and probing on consumer attitudes and usage habits, to identify new insights.
4. **Continue Research:** Ongoing research is critical to really understand whether/how these preliminary insights (and concepts) are shared and viewed as truly relevant, extensive, and compelling. Furthermore, learn how consumers talk about these issues, and continue to seek out the most captivating and meaningful expressions to describe these insights and concepts. You will know when you have found a powerful insight (a) when you can offer a benefit and/or a "reason why" that capitalizes on it, and (b) when it is different from competition and you can deliver on its promise. More research will be needed to

verify that the associated benefit or supporting RTB is truly meaning-ful and shared by enough consumers. Ideally, the new insight will be so novel that you can develop a proprietary claim or benefit that you can actually own. Finally, the new insight and related benefit/support must complement the current positioning and brand personality.

Here is an example of how P&G identified a new insight that led to the re-formulation and re-positioning of Tide years ago, a consumer com-plaining in focus groups using words like:

the kids really get their clothes dirty. I have to wash so often I actually wear their clothes out. So while I can't afford to keep on buying new clothes, I am willing to pay more for a detergent that not only cleans, but also keeps clothes from fading or fraying.

This view was actually an obstacle among cost-conscious consumers for not using a premium-priced detergent like Tide—it simply wasn't superior enough at cleaning clothes to warrant its premium price. Discov-ering this consumer insight, however, led the R&D labs at P&G to develop a new formulation with special degreasers and fabric softeners, so they could offer a new, more compelling benefit: "Tide gets out the toughest dirt while keeping clothes from fading or fraying from so much washing. So clothes don't just look cleaner; they stay newer looking longer...wash after wash." Importantly, this new positioning claim struck the consumer's "hot button" or emotional "sweet spot" and resurrected the Tide brand.

Consumer Insights for Emotional Branding

Identifying and defining a compelling consumer insight that is shared by many consumers is only half the battle. Translating this into a relevant brand positioning with a heartfelt emotional dimension is the other major challenge for marketers. Many categories—premium foods, beverages, services—focus almost exclusively on the emotional rationale for using a particular product.

McDonald's is a perfect example of emotional branding. When you think of McDonald's, most people immediately associate it with its prod-uct or service attributes such as its hamburgers and quick service as its "reason for being." Focusing on these "product benefits" will mean a value proposition for McDonald's as offering convenience-oriented eaters fast meals at competitive prices.

Fortunately, McDonald's has gone beyond these obvious physical functions to brand itself in an emotional way as the ultimate fun experience primarily for families with kids. They have spelled out this target prospect in great detail to create an actionable psychographic profile: "with strong wholesome values, seeking to enjoy the visit and meal, sharing the food and experience, and who want reliable quality and like tasty food at reasonable prices." With this target definition as its starting point, McDonald's positioning statement reads:

> **For:** families with kids (primarily) who want quick, tasty meals and a fun experience, **Brand/Competitive Framework:** McDonald's is the brand of choice among family oriented fast food restaurants, that **Benefit:** provides a fun time experience for kids and their family (the top priority), because **Reasons Why:** it offers (1) fast, reliable, cheerful, and efficient service; (2) food that is tasty, with reasonable pricing/ good value, popular (e.g., hamburgers and fries) and consistent quality; and (3) an environment that is clean, same all over, safe, fun (McDonald's Magic), and family oriented. **Brand Personality:** Like a trusted friend—reliable, friendly, wants to share everything with you, makes you happy, provides opportunity for a "special" time together, wholesome, genuine, honest, and always there for you.

Importantly, this positioning is consistent with the company's overall vision and mission statement, which are also defined with experiential overtones:

> *Corporate Vision:* "to be the world's best quick service restaurant experience"
>
> *Mission Statement:* "provide outstanding quality, service, cleanliness and value, so that we make every customer in every restaurant smile," or put in a more direct way, get the customer satisfied as fast as possible, and to leave just as fast with a happy face

Satisfaction is an emotion that every service business seeks, but <u>how</u> they achieve this will determine how special the brand will become in the minds and hearts of category consumers. For McDonald's, memorable communications and distinctive brand associations have shaped its brand personality and legacy like no other. In the past 15 years, its advertising slogans have changed but they all communicate the consistent emotional brand soul of McDonald's:

"You deserve a break today"
"We love to see you smile"
"I'm lovin' it" (current)

Consumer insights can be discovered in all forms of research; sometimes these findings can be used to reinforce a current brand personality built on an emotional image. In some countries, for example, automobiles are marketed as an analogous tool of sexual conquest. The type of car one drives can also say a lot about who he/she is and how he/she expects to be treated. According to Professor Werner Hagstotz, an expert in automobile marketing at the School of Applied Sciences in Pforzheim, "for Germans, the car is a unique symbol of identity. It's like a bottle of wine for a Frenchman."

So you can imagine the delight for BMW when they learned about the research results from the German magazine *Men's Car*, which surveyed 2,253 drivers between 20 and 50 years of age about their sexual habits. The BMW brand is positioned as the ultimate status symbol, especially for active professionals. These survey results added a new dimension to this brand identity when it revealed that BMW owners allegedly have sex more often than any other car owner, an average of 2.2 times a week, whereas Porsche owners have sex least often, 1.4 times a week.

Types of "Feelings"

Numerous studies have tried to identify and measure the effect of brand advertising on emotional feelings (such as Burke & Edell 1989; Russo & Stephens 1990; Stayman & Aaker 1988; and Goodstein, Edell and Moore 1990). All these feelings were segmented and listed under four types: upbeat feelings, warm feelings, negative feelings, and uneasy feelings. Although much of this may be arbitrary, the following table does provide a useful perspective on the significant variety of different emotions that may be associated with brand personalities:

Upbeat feelings	Warm feelings	Uneasy feelings	Negative feelings
Active	Affectionate	Afraid	Bored
Alive	Calm	Anxious	Critical
Amused	Emotional	Concerned	Defiant
Attentive	Hopeful	Contemplative	Disinterested
Attractive	Kind	Depressed	Dubious
Carefree	Moved	Edgy	Dull
Cheerful	Peaceful	Pensive	Suspicious
Delighted	Warmhearted	Regretful	
Elated		Sad	
Energetic		Tense	
Happy		Troubled	
Humorous		Uncomfortable	
Independent		Uneasy	
Industrious		Worried	
Inspired			
Interested			
Joyous			
Lighthearted			
Playful			
Pleased			
Proud			
Satisfied			
Stimulated			
Strong			

Robert Plutchik, Professor Emeritus at the Albert Einstein College of Medicine in New York and a renowned authority on human emotions, has written a book on this subject of emotional relationships, *Emotions and Life: Perspectives from Psychology, Biology and Evolution*. His theory is that there are eight basic emotions that serve as the building blocks for all human emotions:

- Joy
- Trust
- Fear
- Surprise
- Sadness
- Disgust
- Anger
- Anticipation

Some market research firms such as AcuPOLL in the United States use these same criteria to measure the persuasiveness of advertising (and the brand), which reflects the ability of the advertising to motivate, appeal, and ultimately make the emotional connection with consumers. Acu-POLL uses a proprietary series of questions, which they call "unarticulated emotional elicitation," to measure these results and also uncover the reasons behind the various emotional scores.

Graham Robertson, founder of the marketing firm Beloved Brands, described in a December 2012 blog how the research firm Hotspex has mapped out eight different emotional zones to help marketers identify optimal emotions for brands. These refer to specific feelings that could be used to align a brand to the specific need status of the target consumer and help define the emotional persona of the brand.

1. I feel liked
2. I want to be noticed
3. I want to be free
4. I feel optimistic
5. I seek out knowledge
6. I want to be in control
7. I feel I can be myself
8. I'd like to be comfortable

The specific emotions to describe the above feelings make up a spectrum denoting the range of consumer emotions, as follows:

Exploring consumer emotions

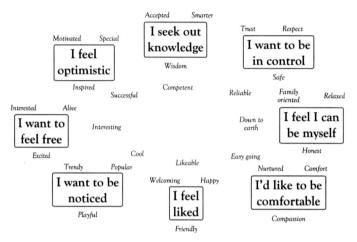

Graham Robertson uses the positioning statement of Listerine Mouthwash as an example of how certain emotions from this spectrum were used—for example, how the consumer wants control, hence the main benefit consisting of confidence, which in turn was rooted in emotions such as trust and respect.

Positioning statement

To...	Healthy proactive preventers, 25-40, who want to do as much for the health of their mouth as they can
	(Target segments)
Listerine is the...	germ killing mouthwash brand
	(frame of reference)
That ...	gives you the <u>confidence</u> of a cleaner healthier mouth
	(Rational/emotional benefit promise)
That's Because Listerine is ...	• <u>trusted</u> to kill the germs that cause the evil gingivitis • <u>respected</u> by dental professionals because it has been clinically proven to be 34% more effective than brushing and flossing alone.
	(Reasons to believe)

The Emotional Branding and Advertising of MasterCard

The MasterCard "Priceless" advertising campaign has become a modern classic of advertising. The favorable recall and attitudes generated by this global campaign reflect the emotional appeal of the relevant experiences and personal values depicted in each commercial. But this memorable advertising started with a major re-positioning effort, involving extensive research, identifying new insights, and adding a crucial emotional dimension to the MasterCard brand.

Brand imagery is the primary driver for all credit or payment cards. Research confirmed that the leading reasons for selecting a particular credit card were related mainly to experiential and emotional benefits:

1. Global acceptance of the card
2. How recognizable and trusted the card is
3. The annual fees
4. Interest rates
5. Reward programs

The perceptions of trust, reliability, and fit with one's own personal aspirations are the key criteria for brand development in this payment card category. Both Visa and American Express had successfully created special brand identities, but until the late 1990s MasterCard had a perception of a generic, emotionally neutral payment card. From a positioning standpoint, Visa targeted itself against the elite "travel & entertainment" with the American Express card as its benchmark, creating an implicit comparison to the more upscale "achiever" image profile of American Express. In particular, Visa had maintained its advertising campaign of "Everywhere you want to be," which appealed to those "bon vivant" consumers who are more materialistic and outer directed. The perceived image of each brand reflected the feelings and aspirations of its target customer base:

Visa: More lifestyle oriented, for those who yearn for the "high life"; more sociable, stylish, and on-the-go; reliable as it is accepted everywhere.

American Express: More professional, for the worldly executive, who desires a special membership, likes to charge as part of their business life.

MasterCard: More utilitarian, unpretentious, used for everyday purchases, practical, less special, almost unassuming.

The dilemma for MasterCard was its lack of a distinctive image, despite a solid base of card holders. Its focus was on the more functional benefits of using the payment card as an alternative to cash or checks, reinforced by its advertising ("It's Smart Money" and "The Future of Money"). This brand message was not motivating and certainly did not hit any emotional "hot button" with consumers. As a result MasterCard's market share continued to decline well into the 1990s.

With new marketing management, MasterCard embarked on a comprehensive research effort in 1996. The main objective was to better understand the current perceptions of MasterCard, and hopefully identify some new consumer insights that would help them re-position the brand. The main findings from this research were as follows:

Changing Consumer Values: The superficial, material-oriented attitudes and symbols for success from the 1980s to the early 1990s were being replaced by more traditional values: being in control, satisfaction with one's own life, cherishing freedom and security, quality time with family, and being able to afford what's really important to people.

Payment Card Usage: Whereas most consumers were aware of the problem of getting into debt, there was an emerging segment that was becoming becoming more careful about using these cards, and felt that only specific purchases could be justified—that is, "not frivolous purchases" or "what I want but can't afford."

Enriching One's Life: Most important, this emerging group of consumers felt more comfortable and responsible using MasterCard for "things that really mattered to them." It was clear from this consumer insight that there was a significant market opportunity for creating a proprietary positioning for MasterCard that leveraged this meaningful "everyday functionality" benefit among middle-American consumers.

The challenge then was how to leverage and convert this potential distinction into a benefit that was indeed more relevant and compelling—to give it some emotional power to get more consumers to feel more connected with the MasterCard brand. The answer was actually simple:

identify a feeling that is emotionally powerful for different consumer segments and cultures, and position MasterCard as the ideal payment card to experience this "priceless" feeling, or "there are some things money can't buy, for everything else there's MasterCard."

The magic of this answer was in how consumers interpret such a feeling, and importantly, how the experience could be enjoyed by <u>not</u> spending money on materialistic signs of success (i.e., as with Visa or American Express). The experience would cost money, but there is no way to measure the true cost of a feeling that can be so emotionally rewarding to consumers. This modified positioning also fits perfectly with the growing trend toward more meaningful purchases to improve one's life. The beauty of this emotional benefit for MasterCard is that even though exactly "what matters most" will vary by consumer segment and country, the associated emotion or joy will always be "priceless."

The Ultimate: Brand Equity

What Exactly Is "Brand Equity"?

It is not so difficult to define brand equity. It is more difficult to develop it and accurately measure it such that it becomes meaningful as a marketing tool.

"Brand equity" is simply the <u>value</u> of a brand, based on how relevant and important all the elements of the brand are, as perceived by its target customer base. David Aaker in his book *Managing Brand Equity* defines brand equity in more detail as "a set of assets such as name awareness, loyal customers, perceived quality, and associations that are linked to the brand (its name and symbol) and add (or subtract) value to the product or service being offered."

Brand equity is an indication of the strength of a brand, or more specifically, how solid and positive the relationship is between the customer and the brand. It is also a sign of brand loyalty, which usually reflects a strong bond with the customer. Like any kind of relationship, it takes time and a well-designed communication effort to cultivate a positive connection.

The first step is to build awareness of the name (and symbol). This may sound like stating the obvious, but it is surprising how many marketers don't appreciate the strategic importance of defining a brand's primary audience, and creating a fully integrated communications program to achieve adequate brand recognition levels, on both an aided and unaided basis.

At the same time, the marketer must create a favorable attitude toward the brand, one that establishes a positive familiarity based on feelings of trust and confidence. This can be a real challenge. From a strategic standpoint, it requires extensive research and analysis to develop a meaningful positioning, which will form the bedrock for a compelling brand personality. Then it takes insight and creativity to develop all the elements of the brand that will make up the net impression you want to make on your customer. David Aaker calls these brand assets or associations. These are dimensions of the brand that all contribute to a distinctive and positive perception of that brand.

McDonald's is a good example of how all its "touch points" are carefully crafted to create and sustain that critical emotional feeling of having a fun experience, the brand essence of McDonald's all over the world:

- Ronald McDonald Clown
- Ronald McDonald Charity Houses, for families to stay while their kids undergo medical treatment
- Appearance—golden arches, restaurant design, playgrounds
- Special promotional toys and packs (Happy Meals) for kids
- Hamburgers and fries—mainstays of menus all over
- Other "Mc…" meals or line extensions—Big Mac, etc.
- Special arrangements for kids' birthday parties

All of these brand associations are designed to reinforce this wholesome, fun image, and also to solidify the perception of good quality and value, which becomes the basis for brand loyalty. The consistent emphasis on these touch points will build brand equity and translate to optimal value for both the customer and the company. For the consumer who will more easily recognize these benefits, their trust and confidence in McDonald's will grow with every visit, assuming of course that each restaurant continues to deliver on its promises of good food, service, and an enjoyable experience.

Brand equity—how is it developed & benefits

The Business Advantages of Strong Brand Equity

For any company, strong brand equity will translate to strategic building blocks for profitable growth in the future: familiarity with the brand, customer loyalty, perception of quality with a competitive advantage, greater leverage with the trade, and financial advantages of marketing efficiencies and higher margins:

- **Brand Awareness:** It may be viewed as over simplistic, but it is critical to evaluate the level of awareness as an immediate indicator of the stage of the brand's life cycle and where/how to invest in the brand's future development. The reality is that often marketers just assume that their target audience already knows about a brand, and want to focus on attitude change or dwell on the emotional benefits of the brand. In "Marketing 101," students learn about the sequential communications process of marketing and selling a product or service, called AIDA:

Awareness ➝ Interest ➝ Desire ➝ Action

Marketing involves the first three steps, enticing the consumer to want a certain product or service, and then sales clinches the transaction with the actual purchase. But the importance of this first step cannot be understated. Understanding the nature and level of awareness is essential for building a brand. This means knowing exactly how familiar consumers are with your brand name on both a "top-of-mind" or unaided (no guidance) as well as aided (recognize name from a list) basis from research tests. The nature of the brand recall is important too. Can the consumer correctly relate the brand name to the right product or service? Is it "Delta" for an airline, faucet, or dental services? As brand equity is developed over time, the level and quality of awareness of a brand will become more vital for adding relevant "intangibles" and associations to reinforce the brand image, for enhancing a positive attitude toward the brand, and for introducing new line extensions from this brand equity platform.

- **Brand Loyalty:** Imagine standing in front of the skin care or personal care section in a Walgreen's or CVS drug store trying to find the right product for your problem. There will be dozens of different products, packages, and sizes in front of you. And you don't have the time, or the desire, to scrutinize the copy for each package. Wouldn't it be far easier, more expedient, and even more comforting to quickly identify a recognizable brand name, including a familiar symbol and other packaging graphics, and just buy that product. This is what brand loyalty is all about—selecting your brand because you trust it and because it promises another predictable and satisfying experience yet again. The stronger the brand equity, the more loyal customers will become, which will create many other important business advantages in the future.

- **Positive Perceptions:** How a consumer views the benefits and quality of a product, service, or company will shape the perceived value of it, the key to building brand equity. What is important is not the actual product quality, but whether the consumer judges and feels that a product offers superior quality, and even more critical, how relevant this perception of quality is to the consumer. It is all so subjective. Positive quality perceptions are also a function of satisfaction with a product, usually influenced by the expectation for performance. A strong perception of quality will create several strategic advantages for a business:
  - *Competitive Difference:* The high value assigned to a product will help reinforce how a brand is positioned so that it will make it

easier and more convincing to establish a meaningful point of difference from competition in the consumer's mind.

○ *Fulfilling a Consumer Need:* How important the benefit or reasons why is for the consumer will help shape the expectations for performance, which must be balanced with the ability for a product to deliver on a brand's promises. Understanding and achieving this balance will provide the basis for a long-term, trustful relationship between the consumer and the brand.

○ *Premium Price:* With a strong perception of quality and a solid brand relationship, a marketer can better justify a higher price and hence enjoy better margins in most cases. (keep in mind the standard definition of "value": value = benefit/price.)

○ *Line Extensions:* This base of strength also provides a sound foundation for introducing new brand extensions in the future.

• **Leverage with Trade:** Like brand awareness, it is hard to generate high-volume trial and repeat purchase unless you have good distribution and shelf presence. Whereas the internet and other direct marketing can help build awareness and deliver a product directly to a household, it will be difficult to achieve a brand's full potential without making it available in recognizable trade channels. Buyers for high-volume food and drug chains, and especially mass merchandisers, are very sophisticated in understanding and judging the potential sales of a brand, and of course measuring its retail performance.

• **Financial Advantages:** A strong brand perception can create opportunities for several marketing efficiencies and profitable results. Once a major investment has been spent to develop awareness and a positive attitude toward a brand, the marketer can focus on a sustaining strategy that builds on this base. Maintaining the core heavy user group is the top priority of this strategy, supplemented by more tactical efforts to expand this base and bring in new users. This usually involves a steady base of advertising and less reliance on expensive trial-generating promotions to sustain the brand, which translates to greater efficiencies for marketing spending and higher below-the-line profitability. Higher pricing can also lead to better margins, another key advantage, assuming a solid perception of the brand quality to ensure good value for the customer.

Measuring Brand Equity

Determining the value of intangible assets such as brands, customer loyalty, and strategic alliances has become a major challenge for any marketing professional, even accountants. Usually these amorphous assets are listed on balance sheets under "Intangibles and Goodwill." In its most simplistic form, such entries are calculated by subtracting a company's book value from its stock price or market capitalization value, or often whatever it takes to make the books balance.

In Great Britain and Australia, which use similar accounting standards, brands are sometimes put on the balance sheet, and their worth is determined independently. In the United States, the Financial Accounting Standards Board is working on rules that would require companies to disclose information that could be helpful in appraising intangibles like brand equity value.

Meanwhile, this quest for a credible valuation model has become the topic of numerous reports and new books, with the focus on exactly how to determine the added value of a consumer brand. The financial community is obviously interested in valuing brands or the "intellectual capital" or goodwill of a company, depending on the definition, for balance sheet purposes. For the marketer, understanding what drives brand equity is critical for the strategic allocation of resources. The measurement of brand equity from either standpoint can be a very useful tool for gauging the past performance of an asset and for identifying new opportunities and threats.

The Economist magazine used a simple analogy several years ago (in 2003) to explain the essence of brand equity. If all the 19,000 McDonald's restaurants around the world, including its frying vats, golden arches, inventory of beef and potatoes, etc., were to burn to the ground, the replacement cost would be about $17 billion. Yet the market capitalization on the New York Stock Exchange was $33 billion at the time. The difference of $16 billion was basically the value of the McDonald's brand equity, which also reflects investor's confidence that the company's value represents much more than the sum of its physical parts.

The value for other famous brands is similarly very high. Dick Maggiore, CEO of Innis Maggiore, mentioned in a 2009 white paper that the portion of the total capital value attributed to brand equity for Coca-Cola is 50% and for Disney it is 68%.

Brand valuation methodologies vary significantly, but like any model, the definitions and assumptions are judgmental. In a 2002 research paper on valuation of brands, Pablo Fernandez at the University of Navarra in Spain summarized seven basic methodologies used throughout the world today:

1. The market value of a company's shares.
2. The difference between the market value and the book value of a company's shares.
3. The same market/book value difference minus the expertise of the management team (i.e., intellectual capital).
4. The replacement value of a brand, based on (a) the present value of the historic investment in marketing/promotion and (b) the estimate of the advertising investment required to achieve the present level of brand recognition.
5. The difference between the value of a branded company and that of another, similar company that sells unbranded products (generics or private label). Prominent consulting firms such as Interbrand use different methods to quantify this difference.
6. The present value of a company's free cash flow minus the assets employed, multiplied by the required return.
7. Based on a brand's strength, calculating the options of selling at a higher price and/or higher volume, or growing through expanded markets and related alternatives such as new distribution channels, new countries, and new products.

For the purpose of further understanding branding as a strategic tool, it is more important to identify and gain a perspective on the inherent market and brand dynamics considered in various approaches for brand valuation. Here are some examples of reputable models:

- **Interbrand:** Calculates brand value as the present value of the earnings that the brand is expected to generate in the future, depending on the following:
  - Projection of the "intangible earnings"—all revenues minus operating costs, corporate taxes, and capital employed charges.
  - Role of branding, a function of the key drivers of customer demand and their dependence on brands.
  - The risk profile of the projected brand earnings, where brand strength is based on seven attributes (with a value assigned to each): market (10), stability (15), leadership (25), support (10), trend (10), geography or internationality (25), and protection (5).
- **Market Facts:** This Chicago-based research firm uses a "conversion model" to measure the strength of the psychological commitment between a brand and its consumers. This model divides a brand's users into four groups, based on this commitment: unshakable, average, superficial, and convertible. It also classifies nonusers based on their willingness to try a brand: approachable, ambivalent, slightly unapproachable, and strongly unapproachable. The difference between the size of the "convertible" for the user and the "approachable" for the nonuser is a significant indicator of a brand's future health.
- **Young & Rubicam:** A proprietary model, the "brand asset valuator" examines the link between the brand and the consumer in two critical areas: (1) vitality, based on relevance and differentiation, and (2) stature, a function of esteem (i.e., when the consumer appreciates a brand's quality) and familiarity. This method only allows a qualitative valuation of a brand, however.
- **Japanese Ministry of Economy, Trade & Industry:** An official brand valuation model that defines a brand as "emblems including names, logos, marks, symbols, package designs, etc. used by companies to identify and differentiate their products and services from those of competitors," and estimates brand value based on the following elements:
  - *"Prestige Driver"*: The price advantage of the brand, created by the reliability of the brand that enables higher prices.

o *"Loyalty Driver"*: Capability of the brand to maintain stable sales for long periods, based on stable, repeat customers (i.e., high loyalty).

o *"Expansion Driver"*: The brand expansion capability, which is a function of the level of status and recognition of the brand to be able to expand beyond its traditional markets into different industries and overseas.

Limitations and Potential Uses of Brand Evaluations

The biggest challenge in any of these brand equity measurement models is accurately forecasting the future, especially the "differentials" (return, cash flow growth, operating risks, etc.). There are many factors that will affect future expectations for a brand, with each one being extremely difficult to quantify:

- Competitive advantage
- Implications from regulations (for brand protection)
- Consumer loyalty
- Emotional benefits
- Brand–customer relationships
- Entry barriers
- Definition of leadership
- Impact from technological progress and new products
- Structure and nature of industry competition
- Company financing
- Brand size
- International stature

By contrast, it can be very helpful for a company to understand what exactly creates value for a brand, and to be able to monitor the progress for brand management. Comparing your brand equity to that for other companies can be like the old "apples and oranges" analogy, as the above tenuous circumstances imply, but the right model can create a value-based brand management discipline that will aid all brand-related investment decisions. Some practical uses for applying brand equity valuation to optimize the management of brands include the following:

- Making brand management more accountable, with performance criteria such as return on investment for marketing expenses and new initiatives.
- Better understanding of how far you can extend a brand asset for line extensions and/or brand licensing.
- Integrating the brand value into the overall corporate planning process.
- Using the brand value as a benchmark for tracking performance (e.g., a brand value score card).

Example: World's Most Valuable Brands (Interbrand)

Using its proprietary model, Interbrand lists the top global brands in the world based on their estimated value. The firm also calculates the percentage of the brand value to the market capitalization value for the given year, which indicates how influential the brand value is to the overall public trading price/value. Because its model consists of financial projections that are constantly changing, the estimated brand values can vary by up to about 15% from year to year. For example, the 2012 listing for the top 25 brands are as follows:

Brand	2012	2011	2010
1. Coca-Cola	1	1	1
2. Apple	2	8	17
3. IBM	2	2	2
4. Google	4	4	4
5. Microsoft	5	3	3
6. General Electric	6	5	5
7. McDonald's	7	6	6
8. Intel	8	7	7
9. Samsung	9	17	19
10. Toyota	10	11	11
11. Mercedes-Benz	11	12	12
12. BMW	12	15	15
13. Disney	13	9	9

(Continued)

Brand	2012	2011	2010
14. Cisco	14	13	14
15. Hewlett-Packard	15	10	10
16. Gillette	16	16	13
17. Louis Vuitton	17	18	16
18. Oracle	18	20	22
19. Nokia	19	14	8
20. Amazon	20	26	26

Note: Criteria for "Global Brand"
• At least 20% of sales outside home country or region
• Publicly available data (e.g., financial data)
• Role brand plays in influencing consumer choices

CHAPTER 3

Branding Applications

Corporate Branding

Role of Corporate Strategy and Values

Peter Drucker wrote "results are gained by exploiting opportunities, not by solving problems." Strategic planning is about the future, that is, the means by which an organization re-creates itself to achieve a common purpose. Planning is really a combination of process and discipline, which are vital dynamics for identifying new opportunities and building strong brands.

Any strategic plan must start with a statement of beliefs or an expression of the organization's fundamental values—its "ethical code." Such a belief should be the basis for the ultimate "why" behind every action. These beliefs must represent a composite of the personal values of those who make up the organization. It should reflect not what an organization is, but what it is at best. It is also the corporate character, indicative of a company's leadership.

GE is a company well known for making its values the hallmark for all strategic planning and guiding its management commitment throughout the corporation. These are based on what GE calls three timeless traditions: (1) unyielding integrity, (2) commitment to performance, and (3) thirst for change.

GE Values—Example:

- **Passion for Our Customers:** Measuring our success by that of our customers, always driven by Six Sigma quality and the spirit of innovation
- **Meritocracy:** Creating opportunities for the best people from around the world to grow and live their dreams
- **Growth Driven, Globally Oriented:** Growing our people, markets, and businesses around the world

- **Every Person, Every Idea Counts:** Respecting the individual and valuing the contributions of each employee
- **Playing Offense:** Using the advantages of size to take risks and try new things ... never allowing size to be a disadvantage
- **Embracing Speed and Excellence:** Using the benefits of a digital age to accelerate our success and build a faster and smarter GE
- **Living the Hallmarks of GE Leadership:** Passion for learning and sharing ideas; committed to delivering results in every environment; ability to energize and inspire diverse global teams; connected to the workplace, customers, and communities in touch with the world

A value system is a declaration of the heart and soul of an organization. It also becomes the foundation for the development and subsequent evaluation of all strategic planning. Based on these values, plus a comprehensive assessment of the market opportunities and internal strengths of a company, a corporate vision and mission statement are created.

Vision

A vision is a concise "word picture" of what an organization aspires to be in the future, providing a clear sense of direction that everyone can understand. An effective vision statement should be simple, motivating, and realistic. It relates to the ideals and principles of a company, reflecting its basic values. Some good examples:

> **Ogilvy & Mather:** "To be the agency most valued by those who most value brands"
> **Walt Disney:** "We use our imagination to bring happiness to millions"
> **Marriott Hotels:** "Every guest leaves satisfied"

Mission

The mission statement is a combination of the corporate vision and management commitment, expressing the strategic "reason for being" for the organization. Like the vision, it should reflect the beliefs of the owners, but be stated more in business terms. A mission statement should not just describe the status quo; it should acknowledge reality yet aspire to the ideal. It must declare the unique purpose for which an organization exists, plus the specific functions it performs. Examples:

Avis: "Our mission is to rent a consistently clean, safe, well-maintained vehicle in a courteous, helpful and professional manner, on a timely basis."

Levi Strauss: "To sustain responsible commercial success as a global marketing company of branded casual apparel. We must balance goals of superior profitability and return on investment, leadership market positions and superior products and service."

Pfizer: "Working for a healthier world"

Merck: "We are in the business of preserving and improving human life"

The personality of any organization is defined by this constellation of values, vision, and mission statement. It lays the groundwork for developing the corporate brand and the framework for individual product/service branding. The perception of a corporation and all its elements must be consistent and credible. Developing a vision and mission statement is similar to the process of building strong brands. These strategic issues must be thoroughly addressed in this process:

Question	What to assess
1. Who we are?	Beliefs and values of the company
2. Why we are here?	Strengths and core competencies
3. Where are we going?	Your vision for the future
4. What we want to be?	Your aspirations and ambitions
5. How we plan to get there?	Opportunity and main products/services

The vision and mission statement provide a dual purpose for strategic planning. First, they become the cornerstone for all elements of the plan: Objectives, strategies, action plans, budgets, and the actual performance should be judged against these standards. Second, it provides focus for the application of energies of all employees of the company to accomplish a common purpose. Just as the company values are the heart and soul of the strategic plan, the brand essence—its credibility and the ability to deliver on the promises—must be consistent with and fit this corporate identity in order to be successful.

Developing the Corporate Brand

As discussed earlier in this "Book," a brand positioning is defined by how it wants all its target customers to perceive it, which forms the basis for a trusted relationship. The corporate brand is the same—the sum total of all the impressions, images, ideas, and experiences that people have regarding the company. The corporate brand, as identified by its name, symbol, color, slogan, and all other touch points, should also be a manifestation of these corporate values, vision, and mission statement.

Every corporation wants to develop positive attitudes by offering an implicit promise to its target audience that it can deliver on and therefore fulfill certain expectations. This is the essence of the corporate brand or reputation—a relationship that is based on high expectations for quality, value, dependability, innovation, community mindedness, good management, and environmental consciousness. The main objective is to create a special impression that differentiates a company from others and is meaningful to all its constituents.

The positioning process is very relevant for development of the corporate brand. It will force management to address the fundamental issues:

- **For Whom:** The target audience and needs
- **Against Whom:** The competition, and how it is different
- **What:** The basic promise or main benefit for the target audience
- **Why:** The reasons why the benefit is relevant and credible

The biggest difference between product and corporate branding is the nature of the target audience. Whereas the heavy or prime customer for product branding can be profiled in great detail and with focus and enough uniformity to create a more concise, special brand personality, the target audience of a corporation is relatively multifaceted. Each diverse group of stakeholders will have different needs and interests, which will potentially affect the perception of a company. The challenge is how to create a specific impression that is relevant for all these segments:

- Outside customers or consumers
- Prospective customers
- Business partners

- Vendors and suppliers
- Investors
- Financial analysts and traders
- Media, national and international
- Opinion shapers
- Government regulators
- Internal employees

A strong, distinguished corporate brand or reputation can have important benefits for enhancing shareholder value: increased sales, market share, increased earnings, and increased stock price. In his book *Leveraging the Corporate Brand*, James Gregory cites the results of his study on the reputations of Fortune 100 companies over time. Those with the best reputations experienced the highest earnings growth and best stock performance. Those with a consistently high advertising-to-sales ratio were considered "marketing oriented" and demonstrated a stronger financial performance. On average, Gregory reported that reputation accounted for 5% of the stock price.

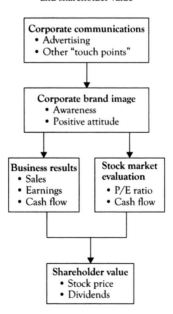

Linkage between corporate brand
and shareholder value

The hysterical craze over rankings in the United States has extended into corporate reputation ratings as well. Every year, The Hay Group conducts research on the most admired companies for *Fortune* magazine. A recent history of these rankings confirms how certain companies are steady performers, while the track record for others is rather spotty, indicating the inconsistency and fragility of the perceptions of these companies:

Rank	2012	2011	2010	2009	2008
1.	Apple	Apple	Apple	Apple	Apple
2.	Google	Google	Google	Berkshire Hathaway	Berkshire Hathaway
3.	Amazon.com	Berkshire Hathaway	Berkshire Hathaway	Toyota Motor	GE
4.	Coca-Cola	Southwest Air	Johnson & Johnson	Google	Google
5.	IBM	Procter & Gamble	Amazon.com	Johnson & Johnson	Toyota
6.	FedEx	Coca-Cola	Procter & Gamble	Procter & Gamble	Starbucks
7.	Berkshire Hathaway	Amazon.com	Toyota Motor	FedEx	FedEx
8.	Starbucks	FedEx	Coca-Cola	Southwest Air	Procter & Gamble
9.	Procter & Gamble	Microsoft	Citigroup	General Electric	Johnson & Johnson
10.	Southwest Air	McDonald's	Intel	Microsoft	Goldman Sachs

Source: Fortune—America's Most Admired Companies (2012).

What is more revealing are the criteria used to rank these "most admired" companies. These qualities range from financial performance to more product and social oriented perceptions like social responsibility and innovation, for example. The top five companies ranked in 2012 for each criterion are:

Rank	Innovation	Social responsibility	Employee talent	People management
1.	Apple	GDF Suez	Procter & Gamble	Apple
2.	Sistema	Marquard & Bahls	American Express	Google
3.	GDF Suez	RWE	Walgreen	Goldman Sachs
4.	Limited Brands	Altria Group	Fortune Brands	McDonald's
5.	Qualcomm	Starbucks	Microsoft	Philip Morris

Rank	Long-term investment	Best use of assets	Financial soundness	Quality-product/ service
1.	KOC Holding	McDonald's	Apple	KOC Holding
2.	Sistema	KOC Holding	McDonald's	Apple
3.	Philip Morris	RWE	Exxon Mobil	Nordstrom
4.	McDonald's	Enterprise Products	Philip Morris	RWE
5.	Exxon Mobil	Philip Morris	Intel	Amazon.com

Source: *Fortune*—America's Most Admired Companies (2012).

The other important advantage of a strong corporate brand or reputation is the use of it as a "parent" or master brand for its sub-brands. With a worldwide market that is growing in clutter and pressure to stretch marketing budgets to be more efficient, the use of such an umbrella branding approach can go a long way to help build awareness and solidify the brand relationship with its customers. Noteworthy examples include Kraft (Philadelphia Cream Cheese), J&J (Tylenol), and Nabisco (Oreo). If the parent brand has consistently high credibility, it can provide powerful leverage for new line extensions, entry into new categories (assuming a good fit), and gaining new distribution in the trade.

The process for developing corporate brands is very similar to that for product or service brands, but the diversity of the target audience for companies makes it important to focus on a very simple, yet far-reaching theme or core benefit for the corporate brand. For American Express, the brand is all about customer relationship. In 1993 when Harvey Golub became CEO, he established three objectives for American Express: (1) to be the best-in-class economics, (2) to provide world class value and service, and

(3) to make sure that every product and service offered enhanced the American Express brand. These principles were summed up by Harvey Golub: "We believe that the brand is our most valuable asset, and that every action we take should enhance its value."

John Hayes, Executive Vice President, Global Advertising and Brand Management, went further: "The brand is the customer relationship: The value of the relationship, the strength of the relationship." It was this belief, that actual product experience would reinforce the customer relationship (i.e., the brand essence for American Express), that became the strategic foundation for launching its Blue Card.

For J&J, the corporate brand is synonymous with "trust." This is the common thread that ties a diverse corporation into one harmonious culture. This core promise has been the heart of a consistent philosophy ever since the CEO Robert Johnson stated his beliefs in 1932 in its mission statement: the J&J Credo. Only 308 words long, "Our Credo" defines its priorities and responsibilities to the (1) "doctors, nurses and patients, to mothers and fathers who use our products and services," (2) "employees, men and women who work with us throughout the world," (3) "the communities in which we live and work," and (4) "our stockholders." This credo can be found in J&J offices around the world and even in every J&J annual report. Strict adherence to this doctrine has enhanced the J&J brand image of trust to the point where this recognizable emotional promise has become the main distinguishing feature for this corporate brand.

Criteria for Strong Corporate Brands

With such a diverse target audience, it becomes more difficult to develop an obvious point of difference for a corporate brand compared to product brands. When you can profile and thoroughly research the core users of a product or service, you will have a better chance of identifying that particular insight or opportunistic "hot spot" that will motivate the consumer and differentiate the product from competition. For corporations, that distinctive brand promise usually evolves from the corporate values, a universal benefit that is relevant to all the target constituents (e.g., "trust" for J&J) and a recognizable, credible strength of the organization.

The emphasis is more on establishing a strategic "beachhead" that can be leveraged and enhanced over time in the minds of all its target customer segments. The key is to build a common attitude and feeling for how a company is indeed special and relevant—that is, to carve out a dominant share of mind and perception of esteem with customers. Here are some important factors that will shape a corporate brand image:

- **Personality and Imagery**: The core brand identity must not only address a meaningful opportunity in the marketplace, but it has to also realistically reflect a clear strength of the company. The same positioning and branding principles used for a product or service brand should apply when developing or refining the corporate brand. Ideally, the corporate name should be perceived as synonymous with a particular aspect of the market and consumer mindset. For example, Volvo is immediately associated with "safety" in the minds of consumers and everyone else. But for their employees and business partners, they embellish their brand identity to ensure that this safety concept becomes the centerpiece for a broader, more fulfilling experiential relationship with all its customers: "style, driving pleasure and superior ownership experience while celebrating human values and respecting the environment." Other features of the Volvo brand identity summary include:
  - *Reputation:* "For safety, quality and care for environment"
  - *Target Audience:* "Affluent progressives who are modern, well-educated, socially conscious, cosmopolitan, active, with a strong need to express individuality yet indifferent to traditional prestige and status symbols"
  - *Key Associations:* Reflecting its Scandinavian origin and values, "nature, security and health, human values, elegant simplicity, creative engineering and the spirit of stylish/innovative functionality"
  - *Tone of all Communications:* "Love of life, humanity, warmth, intelligence, and honesty"
- **Communications:** Effectively delivering the message and creating the desired relationship with all the target groups has become a top priority for corporations today, especially with the great need to

develop more credible corporate governance practices. Since each segment of the corporate target audience will have different expectations and perspectives, the positioning elements (e.g., emphasizing different support or "reasons to believe" points) must be adjusted accordingly in the communications. However, the central brand personality and promise must prevail for all groups. A communications platform must be established which should define for the various target segments:

o Who you are
o What makes your company special
o What you can realistically and credibly promise
o The corporate brand identity and desired reputation

The execution of the corporate brand can be complicated and challenging due to the diversity of the target audience. Fortunately, marketing in general has changed dramatically in recent years, from a mass marketing orientation to a more opportunistic micro or digital marketing practice. The consumer market has become more fragmented, but the means to reach each market segment has become more effective and sophisticated. New digital media (e.g., social media) have enabled marketers to communicate more customized messages to each target segment. Also the emergence of "guerilla marketing" or unconventional media tactics to cut through clutter and reach a certain target audience has added another dimension to the arsenal of weapons for a corporate communications platform. Finally, companies are becoming more expert at "integrated marketing" techniques, where every brand association, communication touch point, and media channel is effectively coordinated to create a single-minded impression in the minds of the customer. The effectiveness of all communications for building a favorable and desired image should be tracked continually in market research too.

- **Quality and Reliability:** This may be obvious but the perception of a company's ability to deliver on promises is absolutely critical today with so many corporate scandals getting publicity. The credibility of the corporate brand is directly related to the expectations for reliable performance and good value. The list of most admired corporations include those same companies that "do what they are supposed to do" year after year. There is no substitute for performance.

- **Continuity and Longevity:** Building a strong corporate brand is a long-term investment. Brand equity is like financial equity for companies. The heritage of a company can be a powerful foundation for developing a trusted relationship with customers, but only if the core brand message remains the same. Communication executions are updated with the ever-changing dynamics of the marketplace, even some of the positioning support elements, but what a company stands for should always stay intact. A good example is McDonald's. It changes its tag line every few years ("You deserve a break today" to "I love to see you smile" to "I'm lovin it" today), but they all consistently communicate the same core benefit of a fun experience.

- **Product Category:** Some categories are simply more involving for various target groups. The perception of a brand can be relatively more critical for establishing a relationship with the customer in some industries, such as entertainment, beverages, food, personal care, and cosmetics, and automobiles. The estimate of the brand equity as a percentage of the market capitalization can be a useful indication of the relative power of a brand in certain product/service areas. Interbrand has conducted research on the importance of specific factors that drive a business in various industries, with the ultimate question of "what would be left if the brand were lost?" This "Role of Brand Index" demonstrates the relative importance of branding by category:

Category	Importance of brand
Perfumes	95%
Soft drinks	85%
Consumer electronics	70%
White goods (e.g., appliances)	55%
Financial services	40%
Hotels	30%
Bulk chemicals	10%

Employer Branding

Employer Branding ... or Corporate Branding?

What makes corporate branding tricky is that there are so many diverse target segments to reach, each with its own interests and agenda. Defining and communicating the corporate brand message to the outside world (customers, investors, regulators, etc.) has of course received top priority attention for enhancing the perceived value of the company, plus its financial performance. The audience, which had until recently taken a back seat, for this corporate branding strategy is the internal employee.

Employer branding (or sometimes called "internal" branding) is really an extension of corporate branding, but directed primarily by human resource management at employees—past, present, and future. In other words, a corporate brand should reflect a company's internal culture; the people at the company will help shape, build, and sustain the brand. The basic objective is the same as all branding efforts: to create a trust-based, emotional relationship and ultimately a loyal, motivated customer—your employee.

The current business climate throughout the world is in bad shape. Corporate scandals such as Enron, Tyco, Lehman Brothers, AIG, and so forth have exacerbated the negative attitudes of the public and employees. In general, many employees feel that they are:

- Over worked and under appreciated
- Disillusioned and disenfranchised by management greed and corruption
- In constant fear of layoffs
- Not receiving enough recognition
- Finding it difficult to balance family and work
- Feeling detached and less trustful of management

Recent surveys support these common concerns. A survey conducted by Interpublic revealed that 62% of Americans say that CEOs are not doing enough to restore trust and confidence in American business, and 69% say "I just don't know who to trust anymore." The *Wall Street Journal* reported in 2003 that 40% of all employees in the United States say they have negative feelings about their job, and nearly one-third of this group are actively looking for other employment (this percentage surely became much higher during the recent recession).

Understanding the value of employer branding is essential for the success of any corporate branding endeavor. The integrity of a corporate brand is so closely tied to the corporate values, and even more important, the ability to credibly deliver on all corporate brand promises. The perception of the brand character and reputation, especially for a corporation, is shaped by the attitude and impression made by every corporate team member, from the CEO down to the production worker on the floor.

In a major research study in 2001, The Conference Board found that over 40% of 138 large corporations surveyed are using some form of employer branding, and this incidence is most likely much higher today. One of the key findings is that a major challenge for companies is to ensure that an employer brand is indeed relevant to the targeted workforce, yet is still consistent with the overall corporate vision, mission, values, and identity. What is more disconcerting is that many companies try to distinguish between the "corporate brand" and the "employer brand." The Conference Board concluded with these explanations for each concept:

Corporate Brand: "Embodies the company values and promise of value to be delivered. It may be used to differentiate your company from your competitors based on your strengths, your corporate culture, corporate style, and future direction."

Employer Brand: "Establishes the identity of the firm as an employer. It encompasses the firm's values, systems, policies, and behaviors with the objective of attracting, motivating and retaining the firm's current and potential employees."

These distinctions are confusing. One of the reasons for this disparate perspective is that the implementers of each strategy have a different agenda. The purveyors of the corporate brand to the outside world, usually the corporate communications or marketing managers, must refine the specific positioning elements for the corporate brand to appeal to the external customer. Meanwhile, the main objectives of the HR manager for employer branding are to help employees internalize the company's values and to achieve a top reputation as the employer of choice for recruiting and retaining employees.

Yet the essence or soul of the corporate brand must remain intact for either the implementer or the user. Elaine Williams from Pfizer, one of the participants of this survey, supported this view: "Our corporate and employer brands are the same. There is one Pfizer brand. I can't think of anything that would fall into the category of 'just an employer brand'."

Developing the Employer Brand

The employer brand by definition is strategic, and requires a diligent, comprehensive effort to develop a meaningful and practical description, in the same way a consumer brand is developed. Most companies already have a stated vision and/or mission statement, which are more business focused— like a vision summarizing the ideals and principles of the company or a mission defining the strategic purpose of its business. For example, McDonald's mission statement is to "provide outstanding quality, service, cleanliness and value, so that we make every customer in every restaurant smile."

The brand essence should be consistent with the vision and mission, and the exact description for the corporate brand and employer brand should emanate from this core brand essence summary, written in a way that is meaningful to its primary customer. Usually, the corporate brand or identity is somewhat general since it must appeal to a multifaceted audience—that is, outside customers and/or consumers, employees, local community, shareholders, investors, media, vendors, employees, government agencies, and so forth.

In contrast, the employer brand must focus specifically on employees, and must be credible, compelling, and offer something to aspire to. A good example is Southwest Airlines, which was a pioneer in employer branding and is known for their excellent customer service. Its corporate mission is "dedication to the highest quality of customer service delivered with a sense of warmth, friendliness, individual pride and company spirit." Southwest captures its brand essence with the slogan used for its external customers, "A symbol of freedom." Keeping the integrity of this image, Southwest extended this slogan to become more meaningful and actionable for its workers, with a new internal campaign called "the freedom begins with me." This enabled Southwest to convincingly communicate that it's more than "a great, fun place to work." The idea was then embellished with a related set of values called "eight freedoms," to show its employees that Southwest provides them with the opportunity to achieve their own goals:

1. The freedom to pursue good health
2. The freedom to create financial security
3. The freedom to learn and grow
4. The freedom to make a positive difference
5. The freedom to travel
6. The freedom to work hard and have fun
7. The freedom to create and innovate
8. The freedom to stay connected

The Importance of Senior Management Leadership

Changing a corporate culture or worker habits is not easy. It requires motivation, hard work, and focus, and no one will do this on their own. This kind of fundamental change will not work if the employer branding plan is viewed as just another HR program or marketing ploy, but will work only if the entire senior management team is solidly behind the concept. The CEO must own, live, and communicate this new employer brand. And there is no substitute for personal contact from the organization's highest levels.

David Neeleman, the pioneering founder and former president of the successful JetBlue Airlines, made it a practice to take a flight once a week and talk directly with its customers. Once in the air, Neeleman announced to everyone who he was and how he was interested in hearing their suggestions. Then, starting from the front row and working his way to the back of the plane, he introduced himself to each person and asked what he/she would do to improve JetBlue if they were the CEO for a day. Not only did the passengers get an impression that JetBlue really cares, but it also demonstrated to other JetBlue employees the true value of genuine and personal customer service—the heart and soul of the JetBlue brand.

Employee Involvement

Great branding starts with a rigorous assessment of the current perceptions, needs, desires, and other issues of the target audience. While the employer brand must reflect overall corporate goals, employees will ultimately determine whether and how the brand definition will indeed stand for something special to them. At the end of the day, employees from every level and function must believe that they can consistently deliver on the brand promises. Most important, the workforce must share in this development process in order to re-establish that essential emotional relationship of trust and loyalty to the company.

Empowering employees to feel ownership of the employer brand is particularly critical for customer service oriented companies. Employees should be given an opportunity to interpret the company brand as it applies to their job function. If they have a chance to refine and improve the brand message, it will be reflected in the employees' attitudes and performance. They will also feel empowered to uphold the brand values and promises, and hence will be able to offer customers more empathy and sincere solutions to their problems—that is, not just lip service.

What Employer Branding Can Do for Companies

Most companies have had an established company or product brand personality that has guided marketing efforts for external customers for years. Many of these companies are now adapting the employer brand to be consistent with the public face of their company brand and customer experience, and to address these critical employee issues:

- Recruitment
- Retention
- Productivity
- Quality consistency
- Loyalty

To return to the JetBlue example, the company was fortunate to recognize early the value of employer branding. It started with the concept of courtesy as the heart of their employer brand and used this to shape and practice their external brand to customers. For example, those crew-members not demonstrating an attitude of friendly, compassionate, caring service in the air and on the ground risk being let go. Gareth Edmondson-Jones, VP of Corporate Communications at JetBlue, said "we wanted to bring the humanity back to airline travel."

The most promising use of employer branding is for recruitment. The personality of an organization should reflect its own people, and similarly the profile of prospective employees should fit this same personality. A good example of using the employer brand to recruit and evaluate new candidates is the on-the-job screening process at the U.K. sandwich chain, Pret-A-Manger. Once a prospective worker has passed the interview step, he/she is required to work for one day in a Pret store. The employees of that store then make the final decision on whether the candidate is hired. This process not only ensures that their new employees have the right "Pret" attitude, but it also empowers and motivates existing employees. The employer brand of Pret calls for employees who are indeed walking, talking brand ambassadors, who embody the "Pret experience," and who can ultimately provide Pret with a competitive edge over other sandwich chains.

Another advantage of employer branding has evolved with the growth of the internet and social media. If the company's brand purpose is under-stood by all, an enormous opportunity arises for empowering employees to use social media and become brand ambassadors. Coca-Cola recognized the power of online and social expressions, and encourages its employees to be active online using transparent, supportive guidelines. As a result, Coke today is widely respected for its open social media principles.

Prerequisites for Successful Employer Branding

Employer branding can significantly enhance the pride, trust, and loyalty of a workforce, which pays dividends in terms of enhanced employee perfor-mance, but only if this discipline is developed and implemented prudently:

1. **Core Brand Definition:** It starts with a clear statement of the brand essence for a company that reflects the corporate vision and values. At the same time, a careful evaluation of what matters most to

employees, their perception of what the core brand stands for, the values associated with it, and their expectations will help create an employer brand description that is relevant and inspirational.

2. **Senior Management Involvement:** Employer branding simply won't work without the genuine, visible support of the CEO. They should "live the brand" as well, and become credible role models for the same values.

3. **Alignment with Corporate Strategy:** Loyalty-based relationships formed with employees should be shaped to deliver on brand promises that are consistent with overall corporate goals, and are uniform across all departments and subsidiaries.

4. **Empowerment of the Workers:** A detailed employer branding blueprint for new HR and communications initiatives, including recruitment and retention programs, should specify responsibilities and accountabilities of key employees.

5. **Ongoing Measurement and Recognition:** Clear milestones, performance standards, incentives, and channels for feedback are essential for success.

Personal Branding

Another area in which "branding" seems to be the panacea for success is the task of a new job search or a career switch. Building your own brand has never been more important, especially as a result of the recent economic recession—business cards, résumés, and even LinkedIn profiles are simply not enough anymore. Moreover, with advances in content management systems, it is easier and more cost effective than ever to build and manage your own personal website. If used correctly, these tools can help you build your own personal brand awareness to showcase what you can do to help solve employer's or client's problems.

The challenge is to determine how to brand oneself to reflect your passions, capabilities, fit with the needs of business, and ultimately become a success in the future. This is commonly called "Personal Branding"—it is what you want to be known for, fortified by the accomplishments that make you stand out. While many celebrities have crafted their own personal brand (e.g., Martha Stewart, Donald Trump), this concept has become common within the context of finding new jobs and career development recently.

Career search has dramatically changed with the arrival of the internet, which has become the major driver behind the need to identify your own brand. While the internet can open new doors of opportunity, many challenges still exist—negative marketplace dynamics, candidate or social media commoditization, and search engine *under* optimization—all making it harder to stand out against the competition. This is especially important for those who haven't searched for a position over the past few years. Factors behind this change include employers who *really* want specific industry experience. Most importantly, your competition is working harder than ever to get marketplace visibility (*Source*: Execunet).

Probably the most daunting question in an interview is "why should we hire you and not someone else"? While many would consider this the ultimate challenge, it is instead an opportunity to communicate your personal brand and sell yourself. How you position yourself and develop an appropriate, appealing brand persona will determine whether your response proves to be a winner. There are two key requirements most interviewers will scrutinize. First, what skills can you offer which will benefit a new company and make you a valuable asset. Second, what kind of relevant experience from previous roles will convince the interviewer that you are more than capable of doing the job applied for. Whatever you say, the tone and body language must be positive, credible, and full of enthusiasm, too.

Any worthy career search process will require exhaustive research and preparation. In particular, developing a personal brand positioning statement can help immensely. This process should start with defining one's vision or goals for the future (e.g., what you want to achieve and be doing 5–15 years from now), even if it seems uncertain at the present time. Then an internal and external assessment will be needed. The self-assessment should identify and prioritize your real (and perceived) strengths and weaknesses, plus your primary interests and passions. The outside market analysis should include the ideal target industry and companies, especially the types of people working there, the corporate culture, and values. If possible, one should also learn more about his/her competition, or the profiles, skills, competencies, and personalities of comparable colleagues working at these target companies. All this preparation should lead to a set of criteria or qualifications for the ideal hire, and then determine if the fit is possible—whether one has the right credentials or can at least convincingly adapt to these personality features to make the perfect impression.

Using a Positioning Statement as Your Blueprint

The personal brand is your promise of value to a target company (the "customer"), so it is critical to shape how you want to be perceived. This is essential for making a lasting impression and developing a trusted relationship, the hallmarks of any successful brand. Assuming diligent preparation, the positioning statement can help develop your personal brand for a better career or job. An example of a possible positioning statement for this is:

> **For:** The target company and their requirements—the corporate culture, values, and types of people who work there, especially the key decision makers.
>
> **Competitive Framework:** Summary of the other people vying for the same job opportunities.
>
> **Benefit/Promise:** What you can do for that company (i.e., your promise of added value) that separates you from the competition and that would be highly relevant to the needs of that company.
>
> **Reasons Why/To Believe Promise:** Your specific skills, experiences, and passions that support the benefit and make your "promise of added value" credible.
>
> **Brand Personality:** A summary of those personal traits that bring this positioning description to life and helps one make an immediate impression of being truly special and the perfect fit.

Similarities to a Captivating "Elevator Speech"

In many ways, your personal brand should act a consistent compass for creating a meaningful dialogue about what you can offer a company, very much like the classic "elevator speech." Peter Helm, a reputable business development consultant from Connecticut for professionals and small businesses, gave this advice for developing a comparable, effective elevator speech:

Your elevator speech is not meant to sell. It's meant to engage. The "speech" (it's an introduction, really) should give the person an idea of what you do. More importantly, it should start a conversation.

Ivan Misner, founder of BNI, says, "The ideal introduction is brief and memorable—one that provides enough impact to arouse the interest of those to whom you're introducing yourself and get them to join your word-of-mouth team."

Here are some "Dos and Don'ts" gleaned from several articles I read recently

DOs

1. **Explain briefly** what you do, whom you work for, and the results you have achieved.
2. Use your introduction to **start a conversation**.
3. Quickly turn your attention to the **other person** so you can learn more about his or her business.
4. **Rehearse** your speech beforehand so that it comes easily. But don't sound like a **robot.**
5. Have **different versions** of your speech: 30 and 60 seconds and a few minutes. Use a version that is appropriate for the situation.

DON'Ts

1. **Pack everything** into the speech. Keep it pithy and short, so it can invite questions.
2. **Use a slogan:** "We're the warm and fuzzy forensic accountants." People will remember you but not in the way you'd like.
3. **Prattle on** about your services endlessly. You want a dialog, not a monolog.
4. **Try to sell**. Focus on the problems you solve.
5. Ask **inane questions** such as "What keeps you up at night?" or "None of your business, fella."

Also, focus on these questions.

1. Who you are?
2. What you do?

3. Whom you do it for?
4. How you do it?
5. What happens as a result?

Views from Other Personal Brand Experts

Other career professionals like William Arruda (founder of 360°
Reach Personal Branding) talk about creating something called "Brand
You"—messaging that highlights your key areas of distinction that can be
conveyed in today's world of digital and social media. In particular, Arruda
describes five key measures of success for building an online reputation
that will help you stand out:

- **Volume:** The total number of responses you can generate, ideally
  appearing on the first three pages of search results.
- **Relevance:** Must be consistent with your objectives and, when
  describing your expertise, position your promise so it is perceived as
  aspirational (i.e., relevant for today and tomorrow), and exude your
  personal brand attributes in all communications like a blog
  or website.
- **Diversity:** Communicate using different vehicles, from traditional
  content (e.g., bio, CVs, articles, websites), to real-time content
  (e.g., twitter), to multimedia such as video, using attractive photo
  headshots in all cases.
- **Purity:** Keep it proprietary yet clean, using your own name and
  removing any "dirt" online that could undermine your image.
- **Validation:** Testimonials and recommendations are critical for
  adding credibility, ideally with a story that reinforces one's strengths.

Another use of personal branding is for companies to assist their
employees to find a role that best fits their strengths and passions, hence
maximizing their contributions in the future. Arruda's 360° Reach offers
a detailed personal brand assessment that allows people to not only identify their most prominent "brand attributes" and skills but also collect
critical feedback and insightful perceptions from those around each
employer.

This original concept of personal branding actually started in 1997, when the famed author of *In Search of Excellence*, Tom Peters, wrote a landmark article called "The Brand Called You" (see http://www.fastcompany.com/28905/brand-called-you). Peters defines a brand in this context as "a promise of value," and he stresses the importance of "selling the sizzle." He advises those in the job market to take an entirely new perspective and to re-position themselves, adapting a similar branding or marketing approach used by consumer product companies. These ten suggestions are still very relevant today:

1. Pretend that you are the CEO of a company called "Me, Inc.," or the head marketer for a new brand called "You," or a free agent who must determine how you will stand out in next season's free agent market, or even a website that is trustful and compelling enough to warrant an immediate response.
2. Identify the qualities that make you different from other colleagues— for example, what you've done lately, your most obvious strength, or most noteworthy personal trait.
3. Develop a "feature–benefit" model for yourself. Knowing the differences is key. For example, a feature of "delivering work on time" will lead to a benefit of the "client getting reliable service."
4. Determine what you can do that will add measurable, distinctive value, perhaps taking on extra projects (moonlighting).
5. Ask yourself what you want to be famous for in the future, or at least strive to become—for example, a great teammate, a supportive colleague, an exceptional expert at something that has real value, or a "broad-gauged" visionary.
6. Build visibility such as initiating freelance projects to meet new people, teaching a class at night, writing an article for a local newspaper, or participating in a panel discussion at a conference.
7. Nurture a network of colleagues for recognition and creating a perception of influence—for example, taking the initiative to write an agenda for the next meeting, or writing a post-project report that can give you more control in the future.
8. Think of yourself as a "marketing brochure" (i.e., not as a résumé) with a portfolio of projects that has taught you new skills, expertise,

capabilities, how to expand your network of colleagues, and lets you re-invent yourself as a brand.

9. Explore new opportunities that will give you worthwhile experience to improve your skills, learn something new, and achieve more.

10. Assess your brand value, check the market, and start interviewing.

Global Branding

Today's Global Challenge—Key Requirements to Win Globally

The world we live in today is visibly different from a few years ago, and not even remotely comparable to marketing conditions a generation ago. The speed of change for communications, connectivity, lifestyles, perceptions, and consumer behavior is accelerating at a stunning pace. While these conditions may be troubling to many marketers, it presents a unique opportunity for the visionary and prepared.

Perhaps the most noteworthy change for business people is the rise of global brands and how this has impacted not only the behavior of the average consumer around the world, but also how marketers must adapt to emerging opportunities for greater scale and profit. One of the first to identify this new "global opportunity" was Theodore Levitt from Harvard, who claimed "Gone are accustomed differences in national and regional preferences." In his famous book in 1983 he projected a vanilla flavored, standardized world—for example, minimal differences between markets, homogenization of consumer tastes and preferences, similar business practices, all resulting in attractive economies of scale and universal brand identities that ignore local nuances.

Fortunately, Levitt's prediction never materialized. Quite the reverse—the global arena has become more localized from a business marketing standpoint. The ideal approach to global success was highlighted in an article featured in 1987 in the MIT Sloan Management Review by Christopher Bartlett from Harvard and Sumantra Ghoshal at the London School of Business, "Managing Across Borders—Strategic Requirements." This was so well acclaimed that the authors expanded the article into a landmark book with the same title in 1998. They described the emergence of a new type of corporate structure, the "transnational," to address the changing business world and global competition. In recognition of the diversity of regional markets, the authors emphasized three basic requirements for global success:

- Global efficiencies from economies of scale
- Flexibility and local responsiveness
- Worldwide learning and innovation

Since then, deregulation, privatization, and information technology have further accelerated changes in the competencies required for success—from a cohesive global marketing strategy to an effective organizational structure to a winning global marketing capability. The most dynamic impetus has come from the explosion of the internet and social media, which has created a sense of collaborative ownership and shared community all over the world. The consumer is in control today. Their demand for full transparency, unbounded access to information, and interactive reach and power though all kinds of new media represent the biggest challenge . . . and opportunity. . . for brand marketers across the world.

The Global Convergence of Consumer Needs and Behavior

The internet has created an apparent paradox for today's brand marketers. On the one hand, the immediate and ubiquitous connectivity worldwide has resulted in consumers sharing the same or at least similar needs and desires, a strong indication that they are more willing than ever to accept standardized global products. At the same time, they want products and services that are more tailored to their individual preferences. In short, you want to be neither mindlessly global nor hopelessly local.

Extensive research by several firms confirms these personalized tastes, finding that online consumers now expect to be offered products that are more relevant and appropriate for their specific tastes. Another contributing trend is the dramatic emergence of available apps on smart phones, which enable consumers to quickly and conveniently find answers to their personal desires.

Consumers around the world have opened up to accepting new types of products, even food and beverages, which have always been categories driven by national preferences. The Japanese are today eating doughnuts, the British have turned to American- and European-style lagers, and people all over are starting their day with a healthy yogurt. A 2009 "Leading Brands Study" by the global branding consulting firm, Effective Marketing, revealed that 69% of global brand leaders agree that their consumers are more global today than they were a decade ago, and 72% also said that globalization will continue throughout the next decade.

There are other key drivers that are exposing consumers in every region to new types of products, resulting in a more uniform, open-minded behavior—easier travel, more handy communications with smart phones, proliferating TV channels on specialty topics. Related to this is the globalization of retail giants like Wal-Mart, Tesco, and Carrefour. Looking into the future, giant retail customers around the world will only get bigger and agglomerated. And this trend will continue.

In short, the world has changed dramatically. While cultural diversity will always be treasured, the trends indicate that the setting is perfect for strong global brands—the growing commoditization of products, the explosion of the internet, the globalization of the media, the increasing transparency of markets, consumers becoming better informed and more sophisticated, and the recognition by investors of the high potential for star brands.

What Is Needed Today for Global Branding Success

A fundamental vulnerability of many global companies is the lack of consistency across markets in brand execution and advertising, best practices, speaking the same marketing language, meaningful return on investment (ROI) measurements for marketing, and an efficient alignment of roles in marketing, sales, and other disciplines. The big challenge for building powerful global brands for these large companies is to align the marketing roles and initiatives across divisions or regions with a single global brand strategy. There are three critical strategic questions that must be addressed for success:

- **Why:** Identify current obstacles that are hindering the journey to global marketing excellence, including key issues like who does what and how do we work more effectively together.
- **What:** The core content, or what a global brand should stand for, leading to a re-positioning of the brand to focus on a single-minded,

universal purpose and experience that is compelling and relevant to all markets.

- **How:** Delivering on this promise of a focused, universal brand requires a corporate cultural transformation, one that empowers an organization with new leadership values and inspires all global marketers.

Country Branding

The notion of "branding" products, organizations, and even individuals has become very popular in the major globalizing economies of North America, Europe, and Asia. No longer a tool just for soaps or toothpaste, this concept now applies to services, corporations, universities, celebrities,. . ., and even countries. Branding is a way to shape a desired perception for a targeted audience so that over time they develop a positive, distinct attitude and feeling for that "brand."

Unfortunately, too many people believe a new advertising campaign or slogan is synonymous with branding. A new ad is simply the "tip of the iceberg." When it comes to building a new image for an entire country, nonmarketing specialists usually consider such a project to be frivolous— and don't appreciate the potential strategic benefits. Good country branding requires much more than a memorable slogan or symbol.

The benefits of a good country brand or image for the client are significant. Given adequate research, solid strategic positioning, and relevant creativity, the citizens of a country stand to gain a great deal from a successful nation branding campaign. . . ranging from a new shared sense of purpose and national pride. . . to increased employment, rising personal and national wealth, social stability, and empowerment. . . to greater individual fulfillment.

For the targeted external audience of a branding campaign, any individual making a decision that involves a foreign country will, by nature, first have emotional issues to address (e.g., trust and comfort). Most often, countries have the three "Ts" in mind as a target: trader (i.e., including investors), tourists, and talent. In particular, the level of confidence and credibility for any business decision will be critically influenced by an individual's perception of that country.

Examples: Successful. . . and Questionable. . .
Country Branding Endeavors

For most countries in the world, the informed global public already has a specific, stereotyped perception. This could be a vulnerability or an asset, depending on the nature of the perception and how it can be leveraged. For example, individuals associate France with elegance, sophistication, stylishness, and sexiness, which are perfect building blocks for French tourism, clothes, wines, perfume, and food. Germany is well known for its engineering capabilities, which has translated well for its premium cars. Japan is today viewed as technically sophisticated, an ideal platform for its automobiles and electronics.

Belgium

Some countries have created a branding strategy and execution to overcome damaging issues and resulting negative public perceptions. Led by Prime Minister Guy Verhofstadt, in 2001 Belgium developed a new brand-building campaign after years of scandals involving government corruption, child pornography, and dioxin-polluted chickens. This led to a new logo, stylish colors, and a focus on its internet suffix ".be" as its international symbol. The intent was to create an impression that Belgium "isn't big, but you see it everywhere you look." Experts consider the Belgian campaign to have been an overall success.

Estonia

After the Soviet Union dissolved in 1991, Estonia was confronted with the problem of lack of awareness among many foreign people, especially non-Europeans. For those who did know about Estonia, they considered it "one of those Soviet republics," with all the negative associations implicit in that. Estonia decided to re-position its identity by associating itself with Scandinavia. Its language is closely related to Finland's and they share many values and cultural habits. . . so this benchmark ultimately helped to differentiate it from other ex-Soviet republics, and establish a new, more positive identity.

In October 2001, Peter van Ham wrote an influential article in *Foreign Affairs* on "The Rise of the Brand State" where he referred to Estonia as an excellent example of a country desperately needing a new brand identity. This was an influential factor for developing the "Brand Estonia" project in 2002 which produced the "Estonia Style" brand book. Its rationale for branding Estonia was summarized as follows: "simply announcing one's existence will not attract tourism or investment; people need to be given motivating reasons for choosing to do business with a country." Estonia wanted to become "The Netherlands of Eastern Europe." It also described itself as "a Nordic country with a twist" and created a public relations campaign that characterized the Estonian people as "radical and reforming, resourceful and environmentally minded, calm and peaceful." Importantly, this new identity enabled it to attract significantly greater foreign investment and tourist flow during the past decade.

Estonia is today cultivating a distinct image as an emerging technology center in Europe. Building on its success developing Skype, a concerted educational effort has commenced to encourage students in elementary schools to learn computer programming starting at the age of 7. It has even coined a new brand name for this endeavor—E-stonia. This effort was initiated by Toomas Hendrik Ilves in the 1990s, the former ambassador to the United States and current president of Estonia, and is supported by a government-backed organization, the Tiger Leap Foundation.

United Kingdom

An essential prerequisite for the success of any country branding effort is to recognize internal strengths that are real. . . and which enable a country to perform in a way that meets expectations based on the branding promises. The style and self-image of the people within a country are critical influencers for shaping a new identity for the outside world. Tony Blair's "Cool Britannia" campaign was intended to emphasize the image of the United Kingdom as a global hub for the media, design, music, film, and fashion industries—that is, to make the country seem hip, enterprising, and cool. This new image has had mixed results, however, simply because most Brits don't regard themselves as being all that "cool."

Nigeria

Another example of underestimating the severity of a country's image problem is Nigeria's "Image Project" initiated in July 2004. Importantly, there must be tangible evidence behind any effort to uplift a country's image—that is, to restore the confidence and faith of both its citizens and potential investors.

In the Nigerian case, the absence of an effective, credible execution has contributed to disappointing results to date. Nigeria is viewed globally as the third most corrupt nation in the world, as a result of mainly bribery in large-scale public projects and the disappearance of several hundred billion dollars in oil revenues. These negatives are reinforced by poor Nigerian work ethics; citizens' dissatisfaction with the government and politicians; poor manufacturing quality; substandard services; continuing ethnic and religious strife; and general poverty, hunger, and homelessness. President Olusegun Obasanjo has made some progress in attracting foreign capital and re-integrating Nigeria into the global community. However, well-intended initiatives like the War Against Indiscipline (WAI) and the National Orientation Agency (NOA) have not been professionally managed and are often used as conduits to siphon away public funds. . . thus turning these very laudable efforts into further evidence of incompetence and corruption.

For countries with very serious image problems like Nigeria, it is best to establish realistic goals, assume sufficient time for changing people's perceptions, provide professional management of reforms, and in the beginning focus only on the highest potential segments of the target market.

Country Branding Models

Successful branding requires a great deal of upfront research on both the target audience and the internal capabilities of a country. Understanding the market and gaining full cooperation and support of key government (and private) officials are essential, before the positioning development and brand marketing implementation can even begin. The objectives of the overall development effort have to be clear, whether they involve the entire country or certain industry sectors.

Here are the five basic steps that we use for our country brand building endeavors:

1. **Client Commitment:** Any brand-building campaign will be doomed to failure if it does not have senior leadership support, if it does not properly reflect the true strengths and capabilities of the public/private society, and if it cannot be properly executed. This can be the most challenging and delicate task, especially for a government-run program, since political issues and internal "turf battles" inevitably interfere with any kind of realistic, honest assessment of a country's strengths and capabilities. It is crucial for the most senior government, industry, or company official (e.g., in government, the prime minister or president) to provide consistent support and unrelenting authority to a trusted manager in charge of such a country branding development effort. A detailed review of these internal resources is a must.

2. **Market Assessment:** "Perceptions are reality" is the watchword here. The target audience might be as broad as the whole world, including the citizens of the client country, or limited to a specific target-country market, or even selected industries or consumer or investor segments within a foreign country. The research should be designed not only to learn about these perceptions, but also to identify key opinion leaders and develop hypothetical branding themes that could become the main motivating force behind a marketing campaign. Depending on the objectives and budgets, this research should ideally start with qualitative exploratory research, followed by quantitative, projectable surveys and/or testing.

3. **Asset Profile for Brand Positioning:** This internal and external assessment should lead to the development of a detailed asset profile for a country or product line, an examination that highlights the most common, relevant strengths and vulnerabilities of that country as perceived by the target audience. Ideally, one should compare these perceptions to a benchmark like another country or the "ideal standard," which would provide a better perspective for understanding the implications. The asset profile is basically a strategic tool for determining the most compelling positioning platform of brand benefits

(e.g., the basic promise or theme) a country could offer to shape a desired image. Since credibility is always a key determinant for success, the support or "reasons to believe" the benefit implications or promises will be critical—for example, (a) will these overcome the initial barriers of lack of trust and confidence... (b) are they really meaningful and compelling..., and (c) can a country initiate the reforms needed to satisfy customer expectations?

4. **Strategic Plan:** How the country brand will be communicated and supported must be mapped out in a comprehensive plan developed by professionals. Targeting different audience segments (e.g., industries to develop or enhance an export business) will require customized marketing tactics and communication vehicles. A multi-disciplined brand-building plan will normally involve advertising (traditional and digital), event marketing, one-to-one advocacy, government relations, public relations, special promotions, and ongoing research to measure the progress. Each function must be guided by this strategic plan. Marketing professionals from the private sector, working closely with designated government departments, should be used for this planning task. Coordination and agreement on specific responsibilities and authority are essential. Ideally, there should be one person in charge of the entire mission, with full support from the president or prime minister of the country.

5. **Execution:** Once the opportunity has been identified and the strategic plan agreed upon, then the creative effort is deployed to come up with innovative devices to communicate and support the new country brand—for example, slogans, symbols, spokespeople, special events, new literature to communicate the brand promises. In addition, the client country's national resources and reforms must be managed in a professional way to show tangible evidence that a country is indeed changing in a positive way. Ideally, national change and reform programs should seem to be spontaneous rather than forced and top–down. This is to avoid undermining credibility in light of perceptions of bureaucratic delays and government inefficiencies. Instead, national change and reform should appear to be a grassroots effort, managed by private institutions, yet with the support and funding assistance of the government.

CHAPTER 4

Building Strong Brands

A Market-Driven Success

The Market Opportunity

Historically, most industries are product driven. Inventors discover new gadgets. R&D labs are pressured to find new cures for diseases. Scientists make incredible breakthroughs constantly in the fields of computer technology. Only the consumer-packaged goods companies have consistently demonstrated the discipline of letting market opportunities shape tomorrow's products and services.

In reality, the development of a brand is not a linear process or step-by-step methodology. It starts with a multitude of different ideas that originate from the outside (marketplace) and the inside—for example, based on the vision, mission, and corporate values and/or a new product invention or improvements. However, as the product or brand evolves, it is critical to thoroughly examine the market at the outset, to create new ideas, to validate hypotheses for brand building, and to determine the market potential for a brand.

Researching the marketplace to understand the optimal brand opportunities should be an ongoing process, because the market (consumer behavior, competition, and category trends) is constantly changing.

Development & execution: Brand marketing

Understanding the market:	Development of business strategy	Positioning statement:	Brand development	Brand marketing
• consumer needs • competition • market trends	to capitalize on market opportunity	How we want customers to perceive the product	How we want consumers to connect with brand	How to build brand equity—create and sustain this relationship

A comprehensive analysis of the market situation is essential, but doing it well is not easy. In fact, the students in my NYU class have more trouble with this important first step than any other. I try to emphasize that a situation analysis does not mean a regurgitation of what is happening out there. The focus should be on what all these dynamics <u>mean</u> for the brand proposition, especially a fresh analysis of the targeted customer—that is, is there a clear market opportunity that the brand can capitalize on? It is really a systematic exercise in diagnostic learning and analysis, the engine for strategic brand creation. The aim is to interpret the external environment, together with the internal realities, to develop unique insights as the basis for creative brainstorming. If a corporate vision already exists, the ideal market assessment will be oriented so that it validates and reinforces it. The following are the key tasks of a typical market situation analysis:

- **Definition:** It may seem obvious, but the market structure, parameters, and main segments should all be clearly defined before other in-depth analyses proceed. There are several ways to segment a market. Ideally, these definitions should be developed to arrive at a relevant competitive frame of reference for the positioning statement.

- **Target Customer:** After concluding exactly who the primary customer should be (e.g., the potential heavy user), determine his/her needs, desires, and problems. In many situations, the decision-making act involves several people or roles, especially in B2B companies. A sense of a hierarchy of these needs, including the hidden wants and insights, is important. What exactly are their expectations today, and anticipated for tomorrow? Often, an additional or second target segment (e.g., influencers) can be crucial for building a brand, such as the medical community for the pharmaceutical industry.

- **Competition:** Who are the main competitors, and what are their strengths and vulnerabilities? How are they serving the market or consumer now? Are there nontraditional competitors who are offering a unique benefit today, or maybe tomorrow, that could become a threat?

- **Industry Dynamics:** Which trends are the most important for shaping the destiny of the brand? Do they pose threats or an opportunity? How will these trends affect the rules of success?
- **Internal Capabilities:** What are the key strengths that we can leverage to address these customer needs and achieve a competitive advantage? Can we deliver on the brand promises? Can we make a profit with the proposed pricing?
- **Strategic Fit:** Is the market opportunity and brand proposition consistent with the overall strategic mission and goals of the company?
- **The Broad Environment:** What is happening all around that may impact the business in the future: economic trends, social habits and attitudes, technological advancements, demographics, government regulations, etc.?

The sources of information for such a market assessment should be as diverse as possible to be able to cover every dimension or interpretation, especially for competitive and consumer benefit topics. Some common sources and types of data to focus on include the following:

- Review of existing consumer-related data
- Search engines such as Google
- Competitors' advertisements and websites
- Online chat room for specific categories
- Ongoing external, environmental, and trend assessments
- Library for competitor information, trade journals, etc.
- Consumer-focus groups or interviews
- Industry experts and other professionals
- Consulting firms
- Sales force and distributor interviews
- Trade associations

The team that conducts this market situation analysis should be multi-disciplined. Marketing and market research should spearhead much of this effort, but it is important to draw on other resources of the company, such as sales, R&D, production, IT, customer service. The main deliverable from this initial market assessment should be a set of new insights, defined as clear and simple diagnostic statements that can be readily understood by all. These key insights have a twofold role: modifying the overall business strategy and providing a foundation for creative ideation for developing and refining brand positioning.

Market Research for Brand Development—The Basics

One of the most common fallacies of marketing is the pervasive belief of "I know exactly how the consumer will respond ...." It is natural for marketers to feel convinced that the consumer will understand and fall in love with ideas that make the utmost sense on a rational basis. The thinking often goes like this: it really is an improvement. I understand and like it and after all I'm a consumer too, they must think like I do. I'm sure they will see this as the key difference from our competition, that the benefit is so obvious that maybe it isn't even worth getting consumer feedback ...

Experienced marketers have all shared such strong convictions, but most have been surprised in the past to discover that the consumer does not always feel the same way. Other marketers, especially those with limited experience, often go overboard and initiate massive studies that generate tons of information, where only a fraction of the results are really meaningful and actionable.

With all research, especially for brand development, it is important to be very clear upfront about what information you need and whether this can be used effectively. The purpose of market research is to assist in decision making, or to reduce the risk of poor decisions. When conducting research on positioning or strategy-related issues, one should keep in mind the many risks inherent in designing the methodology and interpreting research results. Some typical problems or challenges that marketers often face are the following:

- Consumer behavior is so complex that it can be very difficult to measure or project—it does not always reflect the real world, especially for purchase interest ratings

- Research can be biased or compromised to support preconceived ideas or opinions in politicized organizations
- Marketers sometimes see research as an exclusive device to make decisions (i.e., not as an aid), instead of one to reduce the risks of decision making
- There can be too much reliance on the procedures, and not the final judgment and/or action to be taken as a result
- "Must win" goals can be misleading and distort research—should be a guidance for learning, not simply a "pass/fail"
- Office politics can get in the way, providing an "escape" for managers

Essentially, there are two types of research: primary research and secondary or "desktop" research. The latter data collection type is ideal for market situation analyses, particularly when there are budgetary limitations. The internet (e.g., Google), libraries, industry associations, trade articles, and other similar sources can be invaluable for estimating the size and trends in certain markets, identifying the competition, understanding regulatory or legal issues, catching up on current technological trends, and learning about other market conditions. While this type of desktop research is easy and quick, the information is not always current or reliable.

Primary research is customized to provide specific feedback from a target customer group on topics such as consumer needs, usage and/or attitude, new ideas and concepts, positioning hypotheses, advertising, packaging, and so on. This specialized research form is either qualitative or quantitative, depending on the sample size. Qualitative research involves smaller audiences (e.g., focus groups, one-on-one interviews, mall intercepts, brief surveys), so the results are not projectable. The fastest growing form of qualitative research is online testing, which is replacing traditional telephone surveys and mall focus groups. All these types of small-scale research are relatively inexpensive and can be an excellent directional resource for new ideas.

Quantitative research requires larger numbers of participants, usually over 125 in the sample, so that the results can be statistically significant, and hence projectable within certain confidence parameters, depending on the specific audience size. There is a wide variety of different quantitative research methodologies, including general market studies, usage and attitude (U&A) studies, product/concept tests, tracking studies, controlled store tests, advertising copy and packaging testing, simulated market response tests, and so on. These traditional quantitative tests are more accurate for predicting behavior, but they also tend to be very expensive (well over $50,000), unless it is a simple, limited omnibus survey.

Online quantitative testing is an option that is very common today. The big advantage is cost. Depending on the specifications of the target participants, a projectable online test with over 100 people might cost approximately $7,500–15,000. However, there are some risks—for example, the quality of the panel of participants (verifying that the desired customer is actually answering behind the computer, completing the questionnaire), fewer questions, more limited diagnostic analyses, and so on.

"Issues" Should Drive Market Research

When I started my marketing career several years ago at Richardson-Vicks, I was both impressed and confused by their emphasis on the concept of "Key Issues" in all planning. We certainly had not covered this topic of key issues in any of my marketing courses in business school, and so it took me a while to fully understand how to apply this discipline. Management insisted that the issues be clearly defined in a strategic context, and that there should be only a few pertinent ones cited, set in priority of importance for achieving the brand's strategic objectives.

An "issue" is basically a challenge or potential problem facing a business. It reflects a current situation or hypothetical scenario in the future that is important enough to influence the success of a plan. Defining these key issues will help you understand and prioritize the prerequisites for success, often allowing you to better assess the customer acceptance of a change or improvement. In addition, issues should determine whether and what kind of market research may be warranted to resolve these questions. A simple "decision flow chart" can help a marketer design a research effort:

Issues & decisions—market research

Issues should determine if/how/when to do research

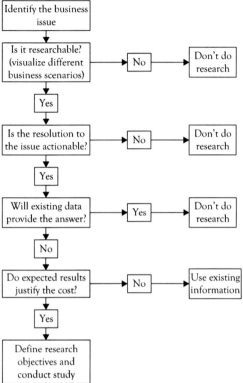

Brand-Related Issues to Research—Examples

Branding is about perceptions, which can make it very difficult to diagnose and reach clear conclusions. Nothing is ever black or white. And the consumer will rarely tell you directly or credibly exactly what you are looking for. Understanding key underlying positioning or brand issues usually involves extensive "trial-and-error" learning and refinements from the qualitative research diagnostics, most often focus groups or some form of one-on-one interview. The experienced marketer will gain important insights and direction using concepts and other stimuli to address fundamental brand issues such as:

• Is the benefit for the brand not relevant, too limited, or just not compelling enough?

- Degree of interest in the core idea of a positioning? Overall credibility of the idea and its support?
- Is the prime target audience profile correct, outdated, or too narrowly defined?
- Is one brand perceived by consumers as too similar to another in a company's portfolio? If so, how should it …?
- Can I broaden the benefit or target base (e.g., with line extensions) without jeopardizing my core users?
- Is there a clear brand identity or personality in the consumer's mind? Is this different from the competition? How?
- Is the current perception of the brand still relevant, or too old, ordinary, or boring?
- Do consumers really understand concepts or benefits that are subject to differing interpretation, such as "indulgence" or "convenience"?
- When expanding to a new market or country, can we still use the same positioning, especially if the consumer values, habits, or needs are so different? If so, how?
- Should the brand positioning change? If so, how?

If carefully crafted with discipline and research, the brand positioning should never change significantly. However, the dynamics in the marketplace can require a brand positioning to be updated from time to time—new competitive entries, technological changes, major consumer changes (e.g., different usage occasions or lifestyles). Also, a brand point of difference may be improved, or conversely perceived as obsolete or no longer so relevant. Volvo, for example, will always be known for its promise of safety, but the reality is that most other cars are now safer as well. While safety will always remain the cornerstone of its competitive positioning, Volvo has added other features or "reasons why," such as style and comfort, to appeal to a broader audience.

Focus Groups for Brand Research

Focus group research is the most common type of qualitative research for getting feedback on new ideas in branding. Marketers annually spent over $1 billion on focus groups, according to *Inside Research*, an industry tracking publication. This form of research is fast and relatively inexpensive, providing marketers with a flexible format to probe for special insights and direction on new ideas. At the same time, there are risks from misusing focus groups—the results are not projectable, and individuals can be influenced by group dynamics. It is vital to use an experienced, objective moderator to control these dynamics and probe for legitimate feedback.

The recruitment is critical for preparing focus groups. At a minimum, you will want the category and brand heavy users to be well represented. Typical qualifications include specific brand usage, frequency of use, age, gender, family circumstances (e.g., with kids), etc., of the participants. Depending on the brand or topic, mixing the groups with different profiles can be risky. In developing countries, in particular, a focus group with people from different socio economic backgrounds is a sure way to curtail any open discussion. When the definition of the ideal target audience is an issue, then several groups will be required to represent the various segments of the overall audience.

Most focus groups start with a general discussion on the overall category needs, usage habits, and attitudes. It is important to not only gain a good understanding of current perceptions of your brand and the competition, but also probe deeper to identify those "hidden" problems or wishes, which can translate to valuable insights for brand building. A good moderator can transform this category discussion into a fertile source for new ideas for brand positioning. There are several methodologies that are used for ideation sessions, which can also be effective for focus groups, especially for drawing out these emotional dimensions and uncovering consumer insights. Here are some examples:

- **Brand/Benefit Laddering:** The purpose is to go beyond the generic benefits of a category and identify those "hot buttons" or compelling benefits that are particularly relevant to consumers. The focus group participants would be asked to "ladder back" from the more obvious functional or category benefits to then reveal the emotional benefits tied to each. These are then prioritized according to the importance to the participants, and become the basis for writing a positioning statement for the top two to three ideas or emotional benefits.
- **Brand Personification:** This technique is used to better understand key competition in a category, by developing descriptions that

characterize the brand as a person. A full line of competitive products is shown to the participants and they are asked to think about each brand as a member of a family, and then to say which they would most likely associate with and why. Participants would also be asked to imagine each competitive brand as a person, and to think about how each person would act in a social gathering—for example, what they would wear, topic of conversation, most obvious personality qualities, and what you might like and dislike about the person. These findings are often transformed into brand archetypes, which help the marketer further understand the perceived profile of the brand versus its competitor.

- **Consumer Story Completion:** This approach enables participants to personalize their feelings about certain issues. They are given an open-ended story and then asked to complete the story on how each issue would be addressed. In particular, the moderator will probe to more deeply understand the needs, attitudes, and emotions toward the specific occasion for using the product, including the perceptions for how each product makes them feel. The entire group then discusses these stories. Examples of types of stories are as follows:
  - Sally noticed that this dessert wine was from Spain, so she expected it to be like _____
  - Mary was in a gourmet wine store, searching for something special to go with the dessert for her dinner party. She chose _____.
  - Mike buys a Sherry or Port for sipping at night, while Nick only buys brandies and liqueurs. Describe each person and why they chose what they did.
- **Collages:** This approach encourages consumers to express their views on brands in a nonverbal manner, by having a few participants cut out pictures from a magazine during the focus group and create a collage that describes the problem or issue for a category, or to visualize what a particular brand means to them.

After a thorough discussion of the category needs and usage habits, marketers will want to focus on the particular issues being tested. For branding research, it is common for the copy to succinctly describe each idea mounted on a concept board, which is like a rough print ad. It will have a headline that summarizes the positioning benefit, a visual that communicates the core idea, and body copy that embellishes the positioning support or "reasons why." It is important to have some kind of stimulus to assess initial reactions and to encourage a full discussion of the overall interest, including reasons why/why not, communication of the main idea, likes/dislikes, product support, and fit with expectations for the product.

Once these ideas have been discussed, the marketer can gain a deeper understanding of the visual direction of an idea by introducing some imagery exploratory stimuli. Normally, these consist of photographs of various product usage situations or other image boards showing some support points (e.g., how a product is made, "beauty" shots that convey certain emotions). The purpose of this exercise is to determine which visual best fits each positioning concept or idea.

Examples of Typical Brand Positioning Issues/Criteria to Probe

General Category Discussion

- User profile, values, habits, and needs
- Buying habits, direct or online versus traditional retail
- Attitudes toward category issues and different situations
- Implications for family, health, social stigma
- Expectations and opinions on different product/package forms
- Perceptions and imagery of different brands in category
- Specific views on your brand and closest competitor

Consumer Response to Positioning Concepts

- Degree of interest in core idea of positioning
- Perception of relative value of a brand
- Overall credibility and relevance of the idea and its support
- Most compelling positioning elements or phrases
- Which ideas best reflect perceived strengths and expectations for the brand

- Which ideas seem inconsistent or in conflict with expectations/ perceptions
- How different or special does the positioning seem versus competition
- Overall favorite positioning concepts, and why

Building an "Asset Profile" Brand Development

Following market research activities, such as a series of focus groups with full discussions of the category, the marketer will begin to see re-occurring themes of similar perceptions or responses consistently appearing in the consumer feedback. The asset profile is simply an analytical tool for structuring the perceived strengths and vulnerabilities of your brand and usually the closest competitor, based on these research findings. Distinguishing between a random, isolated observation and an immediate impression or spontaneous reaction that is frequently demonstrated by consumers can be tricky, however. These same perceptions must occur over and over in research before they can be legitimately classified as a "strength" or "vulnerability."

The main purpose of this asset profile process is to identify those key strengths that can be leveraged for brand building, relative to competition. In particular, the relevant strengths that a marketer will want to identify for his/her brand must:

- Differentiate the brand from competition
- Favorably compare with the perceived vulnerabilities or weaknesses of the competitor
- Identify those vulnerabilities that can be overcome with improved positioning
- Lead to a proprietary or "ownable" positioning for the brand
- Enhance the perceived value of the brand over time

All these research findings are evaluated and consolidated so that the key brand benefits and vulnerabilities can be clustered under types or platforms. Several years ago focus groups were conducted to better understand the core perceptions for the Kodak brand in the United States, as a way to determine the specific strengths to build on for new line extensions:

Kodak's Benefit Platform

Perceived strengths	Perceived vulnerabilities
Quality: • Best film • Best pictures • Best processing • Best paper • Consistency	• Higher priced • Not great value • Lower quality cameras
Simplicity: • Easy to use • Compact cameras • Not sophisticated	• Low technology • Not innovative • Plain
Traditional: • American • Mainstream • Older • Conservative	• Status quo • For conformists • For materialists • Monopolistic • Not contemporary or hip • Not young
Reliable: • Trusted • Leader • Dependable • No worries • Lasts through time • Everywhere • Heavily advertised	• Brainwashed • For the easily influenced
Family: • Mom • Apple pie • Kids • Part of family life • Nurturing	• Not single
Emotional: • Kodak Moment • Expressive • Moods • Precious times • Memories • Special events • Rewarding • Sharing	

The asset profile process is an excellent way to objectively check the current perceptions of a product or corporate brand, which is indeed the "reality" despite what many internal managers may think or wish. This analytical tool is also very helpful for developing the positioning of a line extension as it will provide useful direction for each element of the positioning statement:

1. **Target Audience and Needs:** Help define and even visualize more precisely the ideal target customer: who, profile, needs, beliefs, and values.
2. **Competitive Framework:** Identifying the competitors that your brand best matches up against, relative strengths, and points of difference.
3. **Benefit:** Defines the core idea or promise that would be the perfect fit with current perceptions, and become the strategic focus or vision for the brand.
4. **Reasons Why:** Distinguishes the specific strengths that could be leveraged and make this benefit promise more credible, ideally becoming a proprietary point of difference.
5. **Brand Personality:** Provides ideas for image qualities that will make up the brand personality.

Innovation and Idea Generation for Brand Building

In August 2011, Clay Christensen wrote in *The Economist* that "Innovation is today's equivalent of the Holy Grail ... and business people everywhere see it as the key to survival."

Innovation takes many forms, but all involve creating new ideas, whether it's the "big idea" or several tactical initiatives. Research consistently reveals that 80% of companies know that big ideas are critical to success, yet only 4% think they know how to do this (*Source*: "Big Ideas" by Jonne Ceserani).

Ideation has often been called "structured brainstorming," and is a powerful technique for innovation. There are many traditional ways to get new ideas—suggestion boxes, hiring reputable business gurus, and various forms of market research, for example. However, today's intense competition and the pressure to transform business models in our dynamic global market require more discipline and thought for effective idea generation. It's not easy, and you have to think ... a lot. As Thomas Edison described idea generation in 1929, it's "1% inspiration and 99% perspiration."

Bartlett and Ghoshal emphasized the third requirement—world learning and innovation—for global success in their book *Managing Across Borders*. They argue that this critical competency will ultimately determine the destiny of any multinational, saying "a company's ability to innovate is rapidly becoming the primary source of competitive success."

Creative thinking and ideation must be an ongoing and ubiquitous element of any corporate culture. This discipline of innovation is essential primarily because we are living in a dynamic marketplace worldwide, where consumer habits and attitudes are constantly changing and competition is becoming more intense and sophisticated all the time. In most reputable companies, everyone in the organization is encouraged and rewarded for coming up with new ideas for resolving certain problems, improving operating efficiencies, and/or reducing costs.

Similarly, marketers should always be vigilant of these consumer and market dynamics, identifying opportunities and insights that can lead to new ideas, and/or seeking ways to improve the positioning and execution of their current brands. The main intent of idea generation efforts is to turn needs into ideas. As a key backdrop, it starts with an update of the market and brand knowledge database and a comprehensive assessment of the current market situation and opportunities. This should involve a complete understanding of current customer needs, usage habits, attitudes, category trends, and ideally a gap analysis, and should answer the following basic questions:

- Where are we now?
- How did we get there?
- What did not work? Why not?
- What have we learned?
- How are we doing?

Product Innovation Versus Commercial Innovation

When people hear of "innovation" in a business development context, they immediately associate this initiative with the development of a new product or solving a specific problem related to a particular product or service.

However, the innovation process (including ideation sessions) is often employed for other, more tactical purposes, called "commercial innovation."

This type of innovation is used primarily to drive the growth of a business. Commercial innovation is essentially any initiative that builds on the business and brand equity <u>without</u> requiring a new product technology or reformulation of an existing technology. The key to a successful commercial innovation for sustainable growth is balancing risk, reward, and resources required.

Product innovation usually requires significant investment (e.g., average $100+ million per major consumer product introduction) and has a longer time horizon (2–3 years). Importantly, the success rate is still very low—only 5–10% of all new consumer products are ultimately successful. Meanwhile, commercial innovation offers several advantages over product innovation:

- Leverages existing product technology, so less investment and fewer resources are required
- Faster speed to market
- More flexible and can be localized or targeted for highly fragmented market segments
- More cost-efficient
- Historically higher ROI, net present value, and success probability

Commercial innovation almost always starts with a relevant new insight that when combined with existing approaches and technologies, creates a new business-building opportunity. The actual product or brand is the focal point of all commercial innovations that are designed to enhance the growth of the core business. Here are some typical types of commercial innovation applications that are used mainly for consumer products but are also very relevant for many B2B situations:

- Benefit reframing
- Value reframing
- Brand architecture and naming
- Partnerships and co-branding

- Distribution channels
- Merchandising and point-of-sale
- Package design
- Claims

Five Essential Steps for Successful Ideation

The ideation process is iterative, beginning with this situation analysis, initial brainstorming, researching ideas and hypotheses with consumers, refinement, more research screening, developing full concepts, more research, until finally you have some valid positioning concepts that will guide the actual product development.

To make the ideation process successful, companies must realize that an organized 1–2-day session will require a great deal of work—more before and after. It all starts at the top. Senior management must be committed to the notion of change and understand certain principles and techniques of the ideation process. Here are five critical initiatives that will improve the odds for success:

1. Know Your Problem and Possible Opportunities

Einstein once commented that understanding a problem is as important as the solution. Although many companies realize that new ideas are important, they have not fully diagnosed the real challenges they face for the future, as a first step.

Every business plan will undoubtedly identify some immediate problems and good opportunities to resolve them, but generally they won't address the more strategic, business model issues that will determine its survival in the long run—for example, future competition, category threats, organizational changes, external trends, re-positioning their brand to meet new challenges, big potential opportunities. Understanding the current perceptions of these problems and related opportunities within the company enables management to establish a minimal threshold for creating really bold, exciting ideas that are truly new and groundbreaking.

How the problem is defined is critical. The ex-Chairman of the Michelin Group once stated that "the fact that the initial problem is badly posed is the main impediment to innovation and the growth of a company." Interviewing key employees, analyzing their feedback, and then writing a clear, definitive problem and opportunity brief will provide optimal focus and a realistic set of objectives for an ideation session. Here are some key issues to address when formulating a problem statement, assuming a more technical problem (e.g., reliability of a system or product, often for B2B):

Situation Analysis: Background should be researched to understand original intentions, expectations, performance measurements, key assumptions, comparable systems or product problems, benefits and relevance to the customer, and other insights.

Customer Impact: Who is most at risk, levels of awareness of problem, exactly who is most worried and intensity of concern, any previous requests for fixing, current perceptions and expectations, how does failing performance affect customers and exactly who, how significant, impact on trust relationships with the company or brand, any remedial action taken to date, expected versus ideal status for the customer in future?

The Problem Itself: The dimensions of the issue, how is it diagnosed, main causes, how serious is it, whether fixable, how and where does it occur, measurement, unpredictability, quality of previous assessments, new capabilities needed to address now, any new theories, competitive experience with similar problems, category-wide solutions for similar problems from other industries, generic or specific?

Other Related Issues: Regulatory mandates and risks, dynamics between government and industry associations, public and direct customers, attitudes and expectations, safety issues, how are they measured, cost/benefit implications?

2. Preparation with Creativity—the Most Vital Phase

No ideation session will be successful without comprehensive, relevant, and participatory planning. In most companies, managers are asked to do the work of several employees today and have little time to think creatively. Often, managers come from afar without any prior preparation to just show up for an ideation session, expecting to create a big, "breakthrough innovation," but they only produce ideas that are flat, unexciting, unrealistic, or just too general or ambitious. This is more like a random brainstorming session.

Nurturing Creativity: Innovation is the lifeblood for any industry, B2C or B2B, and creativity is the primary talent for generating new ideas. The significant market and structural changes in both the B2B and B2C worlds demand more creativity today. Most often, high levels of creativity have been associated with B2C initiatives of all types, while in B2B circles this has been focused mainly on product development. A central issue for all is whether creativity is a talent that is simply instinctive or could be developed, and how.

In 2010, IBM conducted a global survey[1] among over 1,500 CEOs, asking what will be needed to "navigate an increasingly complex world." The most important attribute cited was "creativity" (60%). What is disconcerting about this growing need for creativity, however, is the problem cited in *Newsweek's* report on "The Creativity Crisis."[2] This summarized the results of nearly 300,000 creativity tests among children and adults over several decades, and concluded that American creativity has been declining since 1990.

Is Creativity Inherited or Learned? For centuries, conventional wisdom told us that creativity was a magical trait, a product of our genes or family history, a rare genius, and that only a select few are born "creative." In Michael Michalko's article on "The Seven Deadly Sins That Prevent Creative Thinking,"[3] the first sin is "we do not believe we are creative" and the second one is "we believe the myths about creativity." Included in this type of traditional thinking is the assumption that the right brain is the source of all creativity, even though no one really has a split brain as the halves of our brain are connected by an immense structure called the corpus callosum.

In his recent book, *Imagine: How Creativity Works*,[4] Jonah Lehrer says these assumptions are "foolish and unproductive." Jonah's book argues that "innovation can not only be studied and measured, but also nurtured and encouraged." As an example, he cites 3M, which is known for innovation. In his visits to its corporate headquarters, Jonah found employees involved in all kinds of frivolous activities, such as playing pinball or simply wandering around during their regular breaks. He observed that taking time away from a problem can help spark an insight, as relaxing activities let the mind turn inward where it can subconsciously puzzle over subtle meanings and connections in the brain. Related to this, the psychologist Joydeep Bhattacharya from the University of London observed how the brain is incredibly busy when daydreaming, which is why so many creative insights happen during warm showers.

Another example of a company culture and practice that breeds active creativity is encouraging employees to take risks, venture beyond their area of expertise, and to pursue speculative ideas. This approach has been initiated by progressive companies like Google. In particular, young people tend to be the most innovative thinkers in any field, as the "ignorance of youth comes with creative advantages," according to Mr. Lehrer.

***Why Innovation Is So Difficult, Yet* So Vital:** Aaron Shapiro highlighted the risks of complacency in his article, "Stop Blabbing About Innovation and Start Actually Doing It,"[5] where he argues that most companies cannot innovate because everyone is paid to maintain the status quo. "Companies strive to do one thing very well, and as efficiently as possible. Success is defined by doing the same thing you've always done, only better, which will lead to more sales and/or lower costs." The result is that creativity and change are discouraged by time constraints, too many approval levels, and a culture that assigns a pink slip for any failure.

These are very basic, business model problems for a company. One option is to establish a start-up business that is kept separate from the traditional company culture and its inherent deterrents to creativity. Here are some critical requirements for this approach:

- **Setting Goals:** These should be specific and realistic, usually seeking a solution reflecting a detailed, relevant problem statement.
- **Separation:** Must be free of all bureaucracy and office politics, ideally with a location away from corporate headquarters, and a different management allowed to take quick decisions, reporting to a senior-level manager. At the same time, some cultural aspects of the

core corporation should be recognized and leveraged in any new organization, which will also avoid risky antagonism or frustrating roadblocks with senior management.

- **Staffing and Ample Time:** Consistent with Mr. Lehrer's suggestions, the team should be comprised of people of diverse ages, expertise, and familiarity with the company's main business, and importantly work in a very open, spontaneous office environment.
- **Freedom to Fail:** The innovation team must be inspired to try new things without the risk of failure hurting their career (as Thomas Edison said, "I have not failed. I've just found ten thousand ways that won't work").
- **Performance Evaluations:** These should be based on the volume and quality of new ideas, not whether they ultimately succeed.

Ramping Up for an Ideation Session: It is important to change everyone's mind-set going into an ideation session, and have them start creating new perspectives and ideas beforehand so they "hit the ground running." Here are some specific initiatives that will help:

- **Give Them a Homework Assignment:** Ideally, this will encourage them to put themselves in the shoes of their target customer and focus on their perceptions, for example, if possible, interview some customers or create a diary that describes their experiences with a product or service. Filling out a relevant questionnaire on customer perceptions, major challenges and opportunities, external threats, etc., will force them to commit their time and creative thinking on paper. One exercise I often use is a questionnaire that will determine the personal brand archetype of the typical customer, with descriptions that reflect personality traits, not functional elements.
- **Conduct Research:** This could be a survey, some qualitative studies (focus groups?), or internet desk research on emerging trends and competition, taking a "shopping" trip and observing customer behavior first hand, studying competitive websites, talking to outside

experts in an industry, reviewing appropriate blogs on key subjects, and most importantly identifying those key drivers or experiences that invoke the emotion and spirit of the customer.

- **Mind Stretching Exercises:** During the few days before the ideation session, special tasks will help the participants "warm up" their creative energies. Scientists at the University of Washington believe that listening to light classical music is a good way to release these creative juices. One unique approach is "forced perspective," which encourages the participant to look at a thing in a different way. Ask them to start thinking of new ideas, even carry around a notebook to jot them down. Then let these ideas gestate and develop in their subconscious, which holds most of the emotional feelings. Challenge them to generate at least 15 new ideas in the 72 hours before the session. Ideas originate from a variety of unfocused, random situations such as the following:
  - Showering or shaving
  - Commuting to work
  - During a boring meeting
  - While reading
  - While exercising
  - In church
  - In the middle of the night

- **Provide Focus:** The problem/opportunity brief should be circulated beforehand, asking everyone to critique it, make suggestions, and use it as a building block for fresh perspectives. The objectives should be clear, realistic, and simple. These objectives will serve to bring the ideation discussion back to the main theme when wandering too far. These objectives should ideally be posted in front of the room where everyone can see it, as well as including them in the problem/opportunity brief. Importantly, an outside facilitator should probe the viability of these objectives with senior management to ensure that their expectations are realistic and the ideation session is designed properly. Finally, there should be a clear agenda, with enough detail to enhance the individual preparation by the participants, but with enough flexibility to be able to pursue and build on unanticipated directions and ideas.

The challenge is to convert relevant needs into new ideas or benefits. Ideation is a discipline that takes many forms, but the key is to think "out of the box" and use various stimuli to trigger new thoughts and perspectives. Idea generation can be structured to identify and build on a variety of issues and insights such as the following:

Ideas Based on a Strategic Opportunity Area:

- Overall trends in demographics, usage habits, etc.
- New technological advances
- New product types—even from other categories
- Unique local cultural factors
- Packaging innovations

Ideas Based on Category Consumers and Needs:

- Usage habits
- Attitudes and perceptions
- Occasions for use
- Buying patterns—who, when, how, where, etc.
- New emerging category segments
- Specific product problems or insights—not healthy, ingredients in product, sizes/portions too large or small, taste is too, ... etc.

Ideas Based on Brand Strengths (from Asset Profile):

- Image of brand personality qualities
- Points of extreme difference versus competition
- Appeal among different consumer types and segments
- Brand name and logo—connotations for consumer and trade
- Packaging features

Ideas Based on Competitive Vulnerabilities:

- Product taste, flavor, or other features
- Brand personality characteristics
- Packaging

- Trade/retail shortcomings and attitudes
- Parentage, or lack of this
- Origin or heritage
- Pricing implications
- Product attributes—ingredients, good-for-you, etc.

3. Getting the Right Mix of People

Ideally, you should strive to get creative diversity to generate a broad range of distinct ideas—that is, a cross-pollination of different thinking styles, both innovators and adapters, left and right brained, and include the select managers who will eventually be in charge of developing and implementing these ideas.

A common question is what kind of personality or creative skills should you look for when putting together an idea generation team. In general, the following are the most common traits associated with the ideal creative manager:

- Keen power of observation
- Restless curiosity
- Ability to identify issues others miss
- Talent for generating large numbers of ideas
- Persistent questioning of the norm
- Knack for seeing established structures in new ways
- High tolerance for making mistakes and taking risks

Clay Christensen from the Harvard Business School recently wrote a book *The Innovator's DNA*, which lists five habits of the mind that characterize what he calls the ideal "disruptive innovator" (with examples):

- **Associating:** The talent for connecting seemingly unconnected things is crucial. Marc Benioff got the idea for Salesforce.com when swimming with dolphins and thinking of enterprise software through the prism of online businesses such as Amazon and eBay. Christensen estimates that business people are 35%

more likely to sprout a new idea if they have lived in a foreign country.

- **Questioning:** Sharp innovators are constantly asking why things aren't done differently. David Neeleman, founder of JetBlue and Azul (in Brazil), wondered why people treated airline tickets like cash, freaking out when they lost them, whereas customers could instead be given an electronic code.
- **Observation:** Closely related, the knack for recognizing different approaches and forms of behavior can stimulate new ideas. Corey Wride came up with the idea for Movie Mouth when working in Brazil, which uses popular films to teach a foreign language, when he noticed that the best English speakers had picked it up from film stars, not from school teachers.
- **Networking:** The best innovators also tend to be great networkers, hanging around venues or events where they can pick up new ideas. Michael Lazaridis came up with the idea for BlackBerry at a trade show, when someone pointed out a Coca-Cola machine that used wireless technology to signal that it needed refilling.
- **Experimenting:** They also like to "fiddle" with both their products and business models. A marketing manager at IKEA realized the value of self-assembly when he adapted to the task of fitting furniture into a truck after a photo shoot by taking the legs off, and a new business model was born.

4. The Ideation Session

By the time the actual 1–2-day session starts, the participants should be eager to express their thoughts and preliminary ideas. Inevitably, there will be some who view a 1–2-day session as a waste of their valuable time. This is why a convincing, relevant preparation and the shrewd choice of participants are so important. The session should be designed so that the participants have fun, too. Certain games and other "energizers" are always undervalued in ideation sessions. Research has shown that humor and laughter can release endorphins, which help people relax, improve their recall, and subsequently yield better results.

While every ideation session will be different depending on its goals, there are several common elements that should be considered:

- **Professional Facilitator:** Some companies are reluctant to spend money for an outside expert in these "cost-control" times, but it is critical to have a neutral and empowered professional to facilitate (but not manage) the session. Good ideas don't come from deep analysis, but from an environment and approach that breeds openness, curiosity, novelty, fun, and risk taking. An experienced facilitator will have the tools and techniques to keep people generating ideas, even when they think they have run dry.

- **Key Components for Ideation Session:** Generally, the ideal number of participants should be around 8–14, comprising a mix of creativity styles and varying expertise. Having the CEO present can be risky, but if so, he/she should take a back seat or supportive role in the brainstorming efforts, generally adding a constructive perspective or insight wherever appropriate. If possible, the session should be held away from the main office in a well-lit, comfortable room (sunshine is best) with whiteboards or flipcharts and post-it notes, including one or two support personnel to record the ideas and help organize the notes on the walls, and most importantly, plenty of relevant props—for example, competitive products, benchmark analogies, examples of customer feedback or perceptions, novel packages from other industries.

- **The Anatomy of a Typical Ideation Session:** There are many formats for an ideation session, depending on the purpose and who will attend. When the participants have to travel, a session should be designed to last at least 2 days, usually with individual meetings before and after. Typically, an ideation session will start on a Monday afternoon with a discussion of the problem/ opportunity brief, the objectives, and some mind-opening case studies and analogies to stimulate their creative energy. Then a full day of ideation on Tuesday, and Wednesday morning devoted to a summarization with refinements of some ideas, prioritization, and a follow-up game plan (conducted jointly with senior management). Another approach might involve shorter ideation sessions over several days or weeks. For example, 2–3 hours to generate an abundant collection of initial ideas (100+), subsequently organize, and cluster the ideas by type (e.g., new product or package, marketing, service oriented, strategic positioning problem solutions), and then let these preliminary ideas incubate in the participants' subconscious for a while to digest and expand upon. An ideation workbook with these ideas defined in clusters should be circulated for review and additional thoughts or embellishments. After a few days, conduct another "upgrade" ideation session over a half day, to further refine, expand, and narrow down the list to around 60–75 good ideas, for example. This should be followed by further scrutiny, cutting, and prioritization in more upgrade sessions, ideally reducing the list to around 15 solid ideas. Within such ideation frameworks, there are other factors to consider such as the following:

o **Building on Momentum from Preparation:** An obvious starting point is to discuss the fresh perceptions and ideas that each participant brings to the ideation session.

o **Make Ideation Ongoing:** Smart companies recognize that the real value of organizing such an ideation is to change the internal culture, to add creativity to everyone's mandate (Google employees must allocate 20% of their time for creating new ideas).

o **Ideation for Different Goals:** Traditionally, most ideation sessions are focused on new products, but more companies are using this for specific problems and also for strategic purposes—for example, different business models, new growth initiatives, re-positioning their corporate or product brands, various marketing or sales tactics, pricing alternatives to enhance perceived value.

o **Customer Perspective:** Any ideation should be shaped around current and future perceptions from their customer, making sure that all ideas would be relevant for them and competitively distinct. The use of smart market research, past or future, can be a critical building block for ideation.

o **Think Long Term/Future:** Another useful focal point is to ask what the company or product portfolio should ideally look like in

3–5 years. Within a framework of category and competitive
threats, trend-building exercises are invaluable for identifying new
ideas and growth opportunities, especially when the group is split
up into teams.

o **Other Exercises:** There is a host of various techniques to keep the
creative juices flowing, each encouraging "out-of-the-box"
thinking. Assuming the participants include those who will lead
the implementation, simulation exercises that involve role playing
or case studies can be very effective (customized training can be
combined with these endeavors, too).

o **Building on Each Idea:** Usually, the "seed" of an idea is created at
first, but to make sure each can be developed to offer real value,
key positioning dimensions should be added—for example, for
which customer and his/her needs, the relevant benefit or promise
has added value, and the key features that would make this
promise credible.

5. Implementation: Making It Happen

Benjamin Franklin once said, "when you're finished changing, you're
finished."

At the end of the session, a thorough and realistic assessment of the
viability of the ideas is crucial. Then the real challenge comes into play. In
most companies, the best managers are usually overwhelmed with too
many mandates and activities, so the last thing they want is another
responsibility. Such an overload situation will never result in successful
development or commercialization of any idea. It is up to senior management to anticipate this possible conflict and adjust accordingly. The following are some important initiatives to ensure effective implementation:

- **Sustain Idea Generation/Refinement Efforts:** Ideation should be
ongoing. Far-sighted companies often use a special ideation session
as the stimulus for establishing a corporate culture that is more
focused on innovation. A new responsibility like this should have
HR and senior management support, including incentives and
appropriate resource allocation. Because all initial ideas require

further financial and market research analysis, the idea refinement and execution stage should be well planned with a schedule of follow-up meetings and progress reports.

- **Criteria for Judging Each Idea:** Good ideation sessions evoke high levels of emotion, which is important for motivating a team effort, but it can sometimes obscure the harsh realities of product/ service feasibility, market acceptance, and adequate financial ROI. A worksheet with criteria should be prepared before the ideation session to help gauge the true potential as these ideas are developed. For example, some sample questions are as follows:
    - Does it solve a real problem—what advantage does it create?
    - Is the message/image consistent with the brand?
    - What are the risks in implementing the idea?
    - Is the competition doing this? How is it different?
    - What is the ROI? Estimated 3-year monetary payback, for example?
    - What kind of further research or market testing is required?
    - Is there any risk of patent infringement?
    - How do we measure success?
- **Developing and Committing the Best Resources:** At this stage, it is prudent to review all work to date with some kind of written "idea summary" document for senior management to study. This summary should define the best ideas to determine those that are worthy of further investigation and research. Marketing, product development, R&D, and/or technical should be in agreement with this idea summary, ideally with input from other key members of the idea building team. This idea summary document should provide information that would be used for writing concepts and eventually make up a positioning statement. Typically, the following data are included:
    - **Opportunity Description:** Summary of the user and usage.
    - **Core Idea Statement:** Description of the compelling consumer need, the benefit, and the reason to believe.
    - **Competitive Framework/Point of Difference:** The main competitors and the benefit or support element that separates it from this competition.

- o **Summary of Supporting Factors:** Key feedback and how
  it is identified, could come from qualitative observations,
  brainstorming groups, sensory panel interviews, and other
  consumer responses.
- o **Summary of Preliminary Technical Issues:** Oriented to the
  product feasibility and possible options.
- o **Summary of Preliminary Financial Merit:** Category size,
  growth trends, analogous new product success stories, market
  share potential, etc.
- o **Timetable for Concept Development and Quantitative
  Screening:** Summary of next steps, consisting of task and
  due date.

Concept Development and Testing

After the idea summary document establishes the leading ideas to build on,
the next stage involves concept writing and testing. Whereas ideas are
focused on the benefit that meets a compelling consumer need, concepts
go further by including a technical "solution" or how the benefit promise
in the idea is to be delivered (i.e., concepts add the support or "solution"
for how each idea/benefit promise can be delivered). This is the "reason
why" support is also essential for determining the execution or form of
the product.

When you add some "flesh on the skeleton" of the initial idea for a
concept, you are adding to the complexity of the hypothetical brand and
product. It is essential that concept development goes through multiple
refinements with consumer input. Forget the "must be perfect the first
time" syndrome. There may be elements from other concepts that should
be switched and/or combined, assuming the central compelling idea
remains intact. This is an iterative process requiring ongoing feedback
from the consumer. Initial purchase intent measurements can easily
change when you introduce new variables and options in the future: pricing, positioning, new product attributes, new feature/benefit linkages, and
distribution alternatives.

Focus groups are used often for refining concepts. Other qualitative
research practices include customer panels, in-depth interviews, panel

discussions with trade and media experts, and competitive benchmarking techniques. The main goal is to determine the viability of each concept, usually with a purchase intent measurement as the key indicator. In addition, it is important to identify those elements that drive this consumer preference, especially the benefit hierarchy links of the consumer benefits:

- Product features/attributes—what is it?
- Product benefits—what does it do for me?
- Emotional benefits—how do I feel about that?

Consumer benefit hierarchy—an example from the food business

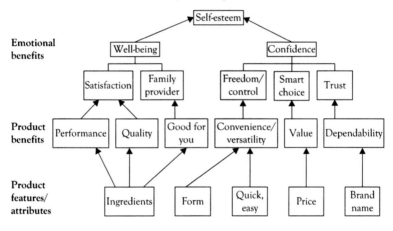

New Organizational Culture and Resources Needed

With senior management's full support, a high-urgency development program must follow the ideation session and extended research activities. This means sufficient funding, selecting ideal HR resources (Peter Drucker stated, "you put your best people on tomorrow's business"), and sometimes customized training.

Steve Roehm from "Strategic Innovation Insights LLC," used to conduct workshops when he was at IBM that focused on this quest of preparing an organization for further development and implementation of new ideas. The biggest challenge, usually underestimated, was how to develop a new business model that can successfully change an organization's culture and resources for adapting a strategic innovation. IBM encouraged its clients to re-assess its organization and develop a new business design for this task. In particular, Steve instructed senior level executives to use a "Congruence Model," based on the book *Winning Through Innovation* by M. Tushman and C. Reilly, for identifying the gap between current and future resources needed for:

- Critical tasks and processes
- Formal organizational structure
- People resources and skills
- Organizational culture

Specific criteria should be established for setting goals and measuring progress, which will ultimately determine the likelihood of success in the market. Key steps for this include the following:

1. Determine the ideal target purchase intent and uniqueness scores, specify trends to be leveraged, re-examine the category size, its compounded growth rate, and competitive threats to the brand, all of which can be measured with further research.
2. Make sure the strategy fits with existing business priorities and core competencies of company, it can deliver against strategic opportunities identified in a situation analysis, it has the ability to enhance total brand value—for example, is it a new category, does it resolve a strategic portfolio or competitive gap, and can it strengthen the competitive advantage.
3. Continually assess the adequacy of current capabilities, existing equipment, the necessity of any process changes, technology within the company or industry, preliminary risks, and other resources needed.
4. When gearing up for an in-market test, set realistic profit targets, sales goals, payback period, contribution margin objectives, and cannibalization losses to be expected.

A summary of this overall innovation model for creating new ideas is as follows:

I. Preparation	II. Ideation session	III. Follow-up
• Target customers + key insights	• Plan proper setting/ environment	• Review immediate feedback & prioritize viable ideas
• Problem/opportunity assessment	• Provide direction & framework	• Create action plan, schedule + responsibilities
• Define realistic objectives & expectations	• Summarize/cluster ideas developed before	• Development teams & allocation of resources
• Competitive vulnerabilities	• Simulations for projecting trends & future	• Criteria for judging all ideas
• Establish decision-making criteria within company	• Use creative ideation techniques	• Roadmap for all research & idea refinements
• Select team for ideation	• Divide into subgroups	• Expand 'seed ideas' into full positioning concepts
• Assign "homework" re: questions & exercises	• Discuss all ideas with others & summarize	• Extend creative thinking to build new innovative culture

Brand Names, Logos, Symbols, and Taglines

Names—the Face of the Brand

Of all the branding elements, there is none that is more important than the brand name. It is the face of the brand, the first indicator of the brand for all awareness and communication efforts. It consciously or unconsciously creates an immediate and usually lasting impression that will shape the perception of that brand. Memorable names will generate associations, which help establish that special meaning of the brand—what it is and what it does, and create a special relationship with the customer. It actually forms the essence of the brand concept.

Today, a good brand name is even more important as it will help penetrate all the clutter that bombards us. It has been estimated that from the time we wake up to our radio alarm, to the time we fall asleep, the average person is exposed to up to 10,000 brand names, images, and messages each day. In addition, the right name will make it far easier to create a distinctive image that will become the basis for long-term value of the brand equity.

Developing memorable names with optimal connotations for a brand has become a big business. Whatever the approach used, and there are many, the same basic criteria should be used for developing a good name:

- **Must Reflect the Positioning and Brand Personality:** Examples of demonstrable names that are very advertiseable: Head & Shoulders, Master Lock, Die Hard.
- **Different from Competition:** Classic example of confusing competitive names: Goodrich and Goodyear. Too close will invite litigation, too.
- **Descriptive, yet Avoid Becoming Generic:** "Lite" beer from Miller is a good example of an unprotectable generic name.
- **Simple, Easy to Remember, and Sounding Good:** Ideally one or two syllables.
- **Not too Confining:** Don't want to describe a specific type such as "Airbus" or "Ticketron."
- **International Use:** The "Nova" car is the popular example of not doing your homework in Latin America (translates to "does not go"). Vicks Formula 44 is another example—"4" implies death in Japan.
- **Avoiding:** Overused names (e.g., Continental, Delta), hyphenated names (Owens-Corning), letter abbreviations (CPC, AMF, FMC, CBI), although acronyms with a certain meaning can be okay (CARE, MADD).

Naming consultants have traditionally focused on semantic associations, or the names whose parts evoke some desirable association. Today, these consultants are going beyond the hybrid versions of new words. A relatively new discipline is emerging for creating new brand names called "Phonologics," which is used often for pharmaceutical products. The purpose is to link raw sounds of vowels and consonants to the specific meaning and emotions desired from a brand. Research by brand consultants and linguists indicate that there is a subconscious relationship between certain speech sounds and emotions, even in foreign languages, which is useful for global brands. For example, the use of "x," "z," and "c" all imply power and innovation. Names with these letters look good in print and people like the sound, especially physicians who feel the harder the tonality, the more efficacious the product is. Examples of pharmaceutical names with these letters include the following:

- Nexium
- Clarinex
- Celebrex
- Xanax
- Zyban
- Zithromax

This approach of "sound symbolism" does start with the brand, or what kind of image the name consultants will try to achieve with a new name. For example, the BlackBerry name fits a desired impression: "berry" suggests smallness, "b" implies ease and relaxation (e.g., won't need a 200-page manual), the short vowels in the first two syllables suggest crispness, the alliteration conveys light heartedness, and the final "y" is a very pleasant and friendly way to end the name. Some other consonants and vowels that have connotations with specially implied meanings and emotions are as follows:

Letter	Connotation or implied emotion
k, t, p	Crisp, quick, so daring, active, and bold (good recall), but associated with unpleasant emotions (also d & r)
z	Most active, fast and daring, yet comfortable
x	Hi-tech action, as with science fiction, cars, computers, and drugs (e.g., "X-Files," "Matrix," "Lexus," Microsoft "X-Box")
v	Also very fast, big and energetic, pleasant emotions
d, g, v, z	With vocal chords vibrating, sound larger and more luxurious than sounds with an explosion of air ($t, k, f,$ and s)
f and short e	Evokes speed and fast (long e implies small)
p, b, d, t	Come to full stop, connotes slowness (vs. z, v, f, s)
s, l	Pleasant feelings (ss connotes "elegance")
b	Reliability
y (at end)	Pleasant and friendly, and is why it is often found in nicknames

The images and emotions that people associate with new names is perhaps best demonstrated in the pharmaceutical industry. Here are some examples of how the combination of the word parts and individual letters can have a particular connotation that reinforces the desired brand identity:

- **Prozac:** The letter "p" implies daring and activity and supports its "ac" ending, which suggests action. The letter "z" also implies action, or speed of recovery.
- **Zoloft:** "zo" means "life" in Greek and "loft" suggests elevation. The beginning "z" and ending "ft" are very attention getting. The letter "z" is also the highest rated for fast and active, yet comfortable.
- **Sarafem:** This comes from the angelic "seraphim," although the ending was changed to "fem" as it is for women with severe premenstrual irritability. This also has a soothing prefix, "sara."
- **Viagra:** Rhymes with "Niagara," which is known for honeymoons, where water is linked to sexuality and life. The "vi" in the beginning is like "vitality" and "vigor," while "agra" evokes "aggression." The letter "v" also connotes speed, energy, and bigness.
- **Cialis:** The "s" sound flows gently, with a smooth "l" in the middle (has no stop consonants like "k" or "p"), so the name is pronounced in a relaxed, open way.
- **Levitra:** Comes from "elevate," with the "le" implying masculinity (in French), and "vitra" reminiscent of "vitality."

Over-the-counter (OTC) brands must be even more simple and memorable as the primary audience consists of average consumers, especially considering the alternative or technical name for each: Tylenol is acetaminophen, Aleve is napoxen, Amoxil is amoxicillin, and Advil is ibuprofen. The letter "l" provides a subconscious feeling of pleasant relief, and so it plays an important role in many of these successful OTC brands. Many of them end with "l"—Nyquil, Tylenol, Advil, and Clearasil.

Symbols, Logos, and Taglines

A brand's symbol and slogan can become important assets if tied effectively to the name. Ideally, the symbol should communicate specific associations that distinguish a brand and reinforce the brand personality. Once a brand has created high awareness and positive feelings from its prior communications, the symbol or logo alone can quickly sustain this well-established impression and consumer loyalty. The brand name "Nike" is rarely advertised today because its "swoosh" symbol is so well known and powerful. And who can forget Forest Gump opening a letter on the stock performance of "some fruit company," with the symbol on the masthead of an apple with a bite taken out of it. The red umbrella of Travelers' is a clear reminder of how this insurance company "protects" and similarly the Rock of Gibraltar for Prudential implying strength and stability. Some other examples of symbols that connote the attributes of a brand: Mr. Clean's muscular sailor representing the cleaner's strength, the "good hands" of Allstate indicating personal care and competent service, and Mr. Goodwrench of GM to communicate its well-trained, professional, and friendly service.

It is important to visually communicate a brand's personality, including the emotional driver that a logo (plus all advertising, packaging, websites, and other brand graphics) should convey. For example, here are some contrasting traits that could guide a brand marketer when creating the ideal logo:

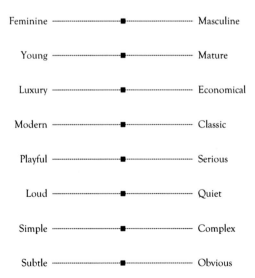

Slogans or taglines are an excellent way to sum up and reinforce a brand positioning. Why risk any confusion or failure to grasp the brand benefit from just the name and symbol when a succinct tagline can quickly capture the essence of a brand. P&G uses a tagline for almost all of its products: "Bounty is the quicker picker upper," "Cascade. So clean it's virtually spotless," "Pamper the skin they're in," and "Dawn takes grease out of your way." Other famous slogans include the following:

- "We try harder" (Avis)
- "Don't leave home without it" (American Express)
- "In touch with tomorrow" (Toshiba)
- "Making it all make sense" (Microsoft)
- "Does she ... or doesn't she?" (Clairol)
- "The best a man can get" (Gillette)
- "The world's local bank" (HSBC)

These slogans are meaningful in English, but they can backfire when literally translated in foreign tongues. The Pepsi slogan in Taiwan "Come alive with the Pepsi Generation" was translated to "Pepsi will bring your ancestors back from the dead." Similarly, the Kentucky Fried Chicken slogan "finger-lickin' good" came out as "eat your fingers off" in Chinese. Some taglines may have a memorable alliteration or rhyme in English (e.g., Pringle's "once you pop, you can't stop"), but often they simply won't work as well in a foreign tongue.

When creating a new tagline, the following are some accepted guidelines to consider:

- Short and simple, no more than eight to nine words
- Communicate or enhance brand positioning benefit
- Paint a "word picture," with words that are easy to remember and that can also be recited
- Original, must be meaningful, avoid clichés, not just "cute and catchy"
- Distinctive, defining customer benefits that set the brand apart from competition
- Persuasive, conveys the "big idea" you want people to know about your business
- Integrate brand name in tagline if possible—for example, P&G's "Please don't squeeze the Charmin."

One issue on taglines that evokes several different viewpoints is whether and/or how often you should change it. Some feel that it should be a permanent or at least long-lasting element of the overall brand design/communication. Taglines from P&G rarely change, as they believe strongly in consistency. Other companies feel a fresh look is needed (e.g., McDonald's third change in five years, to "I'm lovin it"), or that their current slogan is too limiting, especially when a company expands its business or services. Xerox changed their slogan for this reason, from "The Document Company" to "Technology/Document Management/Consulting," which may be a more accurate representation of their new direction but is certainly not as memorable. In any case, the concept behind the tagline, permanent or new, should <u>always</u> reflect the essence of the brand, which should never change. My view: consistency and longevity should be preferred for building trustful relationships with consumers.

Ideally, a good slogan or tagline should be used to supplement the basic brand message and enhance the overall communication of the brand. Here are some examples of specific uses of brand taglines:

Creative copy to communicate benefit

- LIPITOR: "For Cho<u>less</u>terol" (to lower cholesterol)
- Bayer Aspirin: "Expect Wonders" (for several benefits—pain relief, anti-inflammation, heart attack prevention, etc.)

Reinforce advertising campaign dramatization

- Viagra: "Let the dance begin" (supporting TV and print ads showing couple dancing, in anticipation ...)
- Gatorade: "Is it in you?" (for visualization of driven athletes sweating Gatorade out of their pores)

Go beyond benefit, for a "call-to-action" behavior

- Milk: "Got Milk" (since 1993, how milk makes your favorite foods taste so much better)
- Oreos: "Milk's Favorite Cookie" (how milk occasions are best only with Oreos, especially for dunking)

- Aflac Insurance: "Ask about it at work" (encourages nonuser to get into supplemental insurance category)

Multiple meanings

- Tylenol: "Feel Better" (not only physically, but emotionally—that you've made the right decision)
- Viagra: "Love life again" (you can have a love life again, plus you can thereby love life again)

Rhythm—to make it easy to remember/play on one's mind (use of rhyming or alliteration)

- Clean & Clear: "Clean & Clear and under Control" (use of similar "C" sounds)
- Bayer Aspirin: "Take it for pain. Take it for life" (use of parallel sound structure)

Establish an emotional connection

- DeBeers: "A Diamond is Forever" (longest running brand slogan in the world)

Brand names in slogans for advertising

- "Dirt Can't Hide from Intensified Tide"

Double meaning with brand names/slogans

- "Volvo: For Life"
- "Visa: It's everywhere you want to be"
- "Sleepys – for the rest of your life"

Slogans that reinforce brand's strategic benefit

- Corona: "Change your latitude"—benefit of Mexican tropics and can escape from the humdrum of ordinary, domestic beers

- Chevy Trucks: "Like a rock"—benefit of hard-working and dependable, functionally and emotionally

Copy words/slogans to reinforce ad campaign idea

- Polaroid: "See What Develops"—demonstrates photos developing before your eyes, plus the commercial where the husband finds a sexy photo of his wife in his briefcase, enticing him to come home for lunch
- Michelin: "So much is riding on your tires"—our most precious possession (our baby) carried by its tires

Taglines that never delivered on their product/service promise

- United: "Fly the Friendly Skies"
- Chevy: "Start the Revolution"

Another important aspect for communicating a brand personality is the overall design of the name, symbol, logo, slogan, color, and graphics. The goal of any brand communication effort is to create a common, harmonious expression of that brand, which must be consistent in all customer "touch points" (i.e., everything that the customer comes into contact with). This is called "brand harmony." Some examples of touch points that should convey the same brand imprint include the following:

- product and packaging (most important)
- all advertising and other forms of communications
- at point-of-sale (displays, collateral material at retail, etc.)
- trade show exhibits
- website layout
- all contact information—phone, fax, web URL, etc.
- all aspects of retail space
- corporate identity (annual reports, uniforms, etc.)

When developing new communication materials, there is always someone who will want to enlarge the logo, change its look, or even abbreviate the company name. The brand is more than a name or logo; it is the sum total of all previous advertising, customer service, product development, and every other aspect that touches the customer. Brand design consistency is critical because it is the face of a company or product. When you make any change to this look, you are weakening the familiarity and hence the emotional relationship the customer has developed with the brand. Even simple changes can confuse the customer and jeopardize the brand's value. With so much clutter in the marketplace, building a consistent, synergistic theme in all marketing and sales materials will help a company break through and build long-term brand loyalty.

Ideally, every brand should evoke some kind of image or feeling—for example, contemporary, traditional, young and hip, easy-to-use, hi-tech. This same impression must be conveyed in all touch points. A good example of a company leveraging a core visual attribute is UPS and "brown." Its advertising slogan is "What can Brown do for you" and this brand impression is dominant in all its touch points—trucks, uniforms, print ads, etc.

Most major companies have comprehensive "fact books," which detail the precise design parameters for the company and brand name, font style, logo, color (PMS number), taglines, etc., that must be strictly followed all around the world. These fact books even define the brand associations that are most important to consumers. For example, Oreo cookies from Nabisco explain exactly what each dimension of these associations means (e.g., for taste, satisfaction, the filling, the eating experience, and the emotional well-being for the brand).

Growth from Brand/Line Extensions

Leveraging a brand to expand its product line has been the dominant approach for strategic growth in the past two decades. By far, most "new product" introductions were simply new sizes, packaging variations, new flavors, etc. One consumer survey found that 89% of these introductions were strictly "line extensions" of this nature. Only 5% involved entirely new brands, and another 6% consisted of the use of a brand name for a different type of product, generally under a licensing arrangement.

The big attraction of line extensions is the ability to leverage the brand name in a more cost-efficient way, versus introducing a new name.

Normally, in consumer products the investment for introducing a new brand can cost from $100 to $200 million, and the risks for failure are significant. A new product brand makes sense only if it is truly different and offers a compelling benefit that can generate sufficient volume and hence justify the high costs of building awareness and brand equity. How it is sold also makes a difference. Selling it off the shelf at retail requires higher levels of marketing support, whereas a product sold directly by sales people or with a doctor's recommendation (RX or prescription drugs) usually does not involve such broad and heavy communication efforts.

For branded products that are licensed or extensions into new categories, the crucial issue is how far can you extend the brand personality and credibility, or what are the boundaries for umbrella branding. Research is a must for understanding the brand associations or connotations of a brand, with penetrating questions like "what comes immediately to mind when XYZ is mentioned," or projecting from real-life situations—for example, "Jane had just finished her Campbell's tomato juice and felt .... ?" Assessing the perceived differences from competition with brand mapping research techniques will help determine where and how far you can extend a brand name and still remain credible and relevant.

Many consumer product companies are discovering that some brands are so well established that licensing a brand name with certain controls can become a huge source of revenue. This licensing form of brand extensions has become a $100 billion plus business, with very attractive royalties (average of 8.5%). P&G has carefully researched some of their brands to confirm the parameters for consumer acceptance of brand extensions, and whether these new products would even enhance the core brand. For example, they tested the extension of "Mr. Clean" against made-up names for related cleaning applications (e.g., Mr. Clean Magic Eraser for removing crayon marks and other scuff marks from chair rails and Mr. Clean Auto Dry for cleaning cars spot-free without hand drying). Even though some of these products involve a different user segment (e.g., men for car cleaning), Mr. Clean was consistently selected over others as the name most trusted.

Today, P&G generates over $2 billion per year from licensing royalties, mostly to products manufactured by other companies. For example,

- Pantene hair dryers
- Cover Girl eyewear, contact lenses, and hair clips
- Mr. Clean household gloves
- Bounty-to-Go towels (without the cardboard core)
- Vicks Breathe Right strips
- Olay Vitamins, linking "outer beauty now with inner beauty"
- Iams Pet Insurance and Travel Meals, facilitated by a broader re-positioning as a "pet nutrition and health company/brand"

There are some essential strategic issues to consider when developing a new brand or line extensions, especially for the use of "umbrella branding." At a minimum, the awareness, quality perception, and the emotional connections to a brand should be solid enough to use as a foundation for any extension. Other issues are:

- Is there a real consumer need and market opportunity?
- Does the current perception of the core brand embrace and complement the extension?
- Does the extension really add value and enhance brand equity, or detract from the core/master brand?
- Use of corporate brand name? Direct or indirect use of master brand name (e.g., "from the makers of ...")?
- Brand elasticity—how far can you "stretch" the core brand with brand/line extensions before undermining it?

Introducing brand extensions can be a very tricky venture, and history is loaded with encouraging success stories as well as colossal failures. Edward Taubner studied 276 different brand extensions and concluded in his article "Brand Leverage: Strategy for Growth in a Cost-Controlled World" that most fit into seven approaches (with examples):

1. **Same Product in Different Form:** Cranberry juice cocktail and Dole Frozen Fruit Bars
2. **Distinctive Taste/Ingredient/Component:** Philadelphia Cream Cheese Salad Dressing, Arm & Hammer Carpet Deodorizer and Vicks DayQuil

3. **Companion Product:** Coleman camping equipment, Colgate toothbrushes, and Duracell Durabeam flashlights
4. **Customer Franchise:** Visa travelers checks and Gerber baby clothes
5. **Expertise:** Honda's experience in small motors—for lawn mowers
6. **Benefit/Attribute/Feature:** Ivory "mild" shampoo, Sunkist Vitamin C tablets, and Gillette's Dry Look line
7. **Designer or Ethnic Image:** Pierre Cardin wallets, Porsche sunglasses, Benihana frozen entrées, and Ragú pasta

The central issue when considering any kind of brand or line extension is whether the current perception of the core brand would embrace or complement the new product. Building an asset profile for a brand is a good way to understand and document the perceived strengths that could become relevant building blocks for such an extension. In his book, *Managing Brand Equity*, David Aaker discusses the key criteria for brand extensions: awareness level, perceived quality, and other distinct brand associations. Aaker categorizes all brand extensions into groups of "the good, the bad and the ugly":

- **The Ideal or "More Good":** This involves relevant extensions that not only benefit from the associations of the core brand but actually enhance it by reinforcing its image. A good example is the "Weight Watchers" brand, where a new line of diet products achieved instant credibility and even increased the brand's visibility and strengthened the main associations of the Weight Watchers program.
- **The Good:** When a brand name provides added value for the extension, by achieving the three main criteria for success:
  - *Awareness:* A high level of recognition of the master brand is worth its weight in gold for a new line extension. It cost over $200 million just to make people aware of the change from Esso to Exxon. The use of a recognized brand name, such as Arm & Hammer with an unaided awareness level of over 90%, will automatically enhance the name recognition of the extension and minimize the marketing investment to establish its presence.
  - *Perceived Quality:* This is the most common association identified by business managers for their brand's main sustainable

competitive advantage. Strong corporate reputations (e.g., for GE, Kraft, and HP) can provide this feeling of high quality and added value for brand extensions.

- ○ *Brand Associations:* The credibility of an extension will be enhanced if it can build on a recognizable feature or benefit of the core brand. For example, Hiram Walker used the Häagen-Dazs name on a new liqueur to communicate a rich and creamy taste, an obvious characteristic and association of this super premium ice cream.

- **The Bad:** Often an extension falls short because the master brand name offers no obvious benefit or added value, especially in very competitive categories. The master brand may have strong name recognition and quality perceptions, but the fit for the extension may not be credible. It has to have the right brand associations, which should communicate a competitive advantage. Campbell Soup was perceived as too watery and "soupy" for a new line of spaghetti sauce, so they had to add a new brand name—Prego. Pricing and the brand image are important too. Timex found that expensive line extensions would not be a good fit, so they focused only on introductions that were very functional—flashlights, calculators, and batteries. On the other hand, Rolex realized its perceived strength was in the prestigious or status sector, which permitted extensions such as bracelets, neckties, and cufflinks.

- **The Ugly:** A major risk is when the extension has associations that are in conflict with the core brand, and ends up damaging its brand image. Other times, there can be so many brand extensions that consumers and the trade may view this as a case of overproliferation, which could dilute the special meaning of the original brand platform. When I was at Church & Dwight, maker of Arm & Hammer, there was great pressure to introduce several new extensions based on the numerous uses of the basic Baking Soda product. The product quality of each was comparable to competition, at best, but we learned from consumer research that the perceived function and benefits were inconsistent with their expectations and many stretched the credibility and integrity of the Arm & Hammer brand name, by far the most important asset of the company. We re-grouped and concluded that any new extension should stay within the functional boundaries of the Arm & Hammer brand, as viewed by consumers: cleaning and deodorizing. In another case, Gillette experienced cannibalization when it introduced a line of low-end shaving creams as an extension of its "Good News" low-priced razor blades. By adding its core brand name to this (by Gillette), however, consumers ended up switching from the main Gillette shaving cream line since they assumed it had the same high quality.

- **More Ugly:** The worst case scenario is when an extension not only causes damage to the core brand, but also gives up an opportunity to capitalize on a solid market opportunity. When Sears re-positioned itself years ago as the "all-in-one" retail outlet by introducing its Sears Financial Network services, the fit was obviously not appropriate and hurt its retail image of good value. Sometimes a more meaningful name is warranted for an innovative new product. "Dustbuster" was the perfect sub-brand name for Black & Decker, versus the bland option of "Black & Decker's Portable Vacuum." It immediately communicated its cleaning effectiveness and helped to create strong customer loyalty in an emerging market segment.

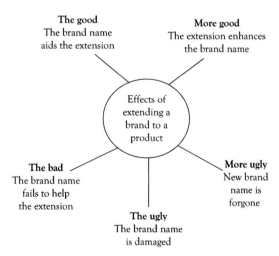

Using the Parent Brand for Brand/Line Extensions

The use and juxtaposition of a parent or corporate brand for extensions is becoming more of an issue for marketers in light of the heavy costs of developing an entirely new brand. Clearly, there are some serious risks for the master brand, especially in health-oriented industries such as the pharmaceutical business. Any problem in the market can have a severe effect on all other line extensions with the parent brand name as well, especially if it is closely tied to the line extension. The alleged sudden-acceleration problem with the Audi 5000 cars years ago had a major impact on sales of the Audi 4000 (–7.3% and –9.6%, respectively), whereas the Audi Quattro suffered by only 4.6%. The "Quattro" in the latter part of the brand name helped separate it from the Audi master brand, and most of its ads never mentioned the Audi parentage.

As in new product development, a comprehensive understanding of the market is an important first step. This should involve a segmentation analysis of the market to determine whether a new brand name is warranted, and if not, how to use the parent brand for an extension, using fundamental strategic criteria like:

- Market potential of the segment. If limited, lean toward a line extension.
- Impact on the core or parent brand. Ideally, the extension should reinforce and build on the same brand associations and offer a competitive advantage.
- Price/value. The perception of value and actual price level will always be a key consideration. Ideally, an extension should be at the same level.
- Possible cannibalization. Unless an extension is clearly separated from the parent brand and offers a distinctive benefit, there will always be some erosion of the base brand business.
- Impact on trade. There is limited shelf space and the trade has become very concerned about brand proliferation. Retailers are increasingly reluctant to allocate facings for extensions with only marginal differences and minor expansion of net sales.

One of the more highly segmented industries is the hotel business, which has created opportunities for the major hotel companies to introduce separate types of hotel chains, each with a different brand name, to fit each segment. The underlying need or brand consideration for all hotels is <u>trust</u>—that is, can the hotel consistently deliver a dependable product fit for the traveler who has different needs? For example, here are some segments of traveler types and needs in the hotel industry:

Customer types	Customer-related needs/characteristics
1. Family vacationers	Couples and single parents with children who want a fun family experience; young, active, and energetic
2. Upscale executives	Senior business executives with a big expense account who want to be "pampered" with "very important person" service and accommodations
3. Budget-oriented travelers	Young people, retired couples, and salespeople who travel by car, pay their own expenses, and want a simple place to stay for one night—before moving on
4. Long-stay guests	Business people, out-of-town visitors, and others who stay in the same motel for a week or more, want many of the comforts they have at home
5. Event-centered visitors	Individuals who are attending events, scheduled at the motel (a business meeting or conference, family reunion, etc.), often for several days
6. Resort seekers	Sophisticated couples with leisure time to relax and have "adult" fun; they want to show their individuality and have discretionary income to spend

Brand Architecture

The concept of brand architecture has become increasingly important as a strategic tool for optimizing a company's line of products. Essentially, it refers to the structure of a brand portfolio that specifies the strategic role of different brands and the relationship among the various brands. Its purpose is to make sure that there is enough "daylight" for each brand in the portfolio, its role and relationship to other portfolio brands are clear, and to help determine which brands offer significant strategic potential and warrant further investments. The basic types of brand architecture are:

- **Parent Dominated Brands:** New products are introduced under a strong, overall brand identity of the organization. For example, GE refrigerators that include the "GE Monogram" and "GE Profile."

- **Parent Endorsed Brands:** New brands with their own identity but with a visible endorsement from the parent. For example, iPod and Macintosh from Apple.
- **Parent Silent Brands:** Brands that depend entirely on their own brand creation and support in the marketplace (e.g., like a "House of Brands"). The best example is P&G with "silo" type brands such as Tide, Crest, Olay, Pampers.

In practice, structuring a brand architecture properly can clarify the potential of a brand and help a marketer determine future strategic initiatives. Here are some examples of various issues that might require a change in the brand architecture and future:

- **New Product or Line Extension:** For example, whether/how to separate to best maximize technological innovations (Apple—iPod, iTunes, iPhone, iPad)
- **Dilution from "Brand Stretching":** With too many line extensions (Spandex Rule)—for example, "Special K" realized it had too many cereal bars under its core brand name
- **Reaching New Market Segments:** For example, realizing the potential of a new segment, yet with concern over a possible conflict with its core brand personality, Disney used Touchstone and Miramax for older movie audiences not interested in G-rated movies
- **Brand Proliferation:** When there are too many brands and sub-brands, and none are unique enough, marketing budgets become too thin to promote each one
- **Acquisition and Merger:** To avoid redundancy, eliminate one of the brands (e.g., Sprint dropping Nextel and AT&T dropping Cingular)
- **Name Misalignment:** Sometimes needing a new name to compete more directly in a different category (e.g., Kraft with "Mondelez" to compete in snack foods against Frito-Lay)
- **Make the Master Brand More Distinct:** When the same company and product names are used too often in communications (e.g., Kellogg consolidating 42 company websites)
- **Losing Relevance:** When a brand is at the end of its life cycle (Oldsmobile), it is best to eliminate it and free up resources

- **Too Many Branded Features:** When an ad or logo includes a company name, brand name, sub-brand, partner name, and a flavor, all in one

The types of brand architecture vary, ranging from corporate dominant to brand dominant, with some mixed brands in between. Here are some examples that demonstrate this wide spectrum of types:

Brand type	Examples	Strategic rationale
Corporate brand (also "manufacturer brand")	BMW Heinz Quaker GE	Strong corporate image is synonymous with product class. Not that common in shelf goods, becoming more popular with technology firms
Licensed brand	Calvin Klein Guess	Used in "lifestyle branding"— for fashion industry, with line extensions in other areas (e.g., sunglasses, umbrellas)
House brand (also "family brand" "distributor brand," "store brand")	Buick Cadillac Green Giant Sara Lee	Common for different product classes/subsidiaries of specific target market segments
Dual brands (also "family brands," "endorser brands")	Sears Diehard Ford Mustang General Mills Cheerios Clairol Herbal Essence	Corporate brand with sub-brand, which can then become umbrella names for product extensions (40 Cheerios types)
Co-brands (also "composite brands" and "ingredient brands")	Ben & Jerry's Heath Bar Crunch Ice Cream Pop Tarts w/ Smuckers Betty Crocker Brownies w/ Hershey's Syrup	Synergistic benefits of each by enhancing perception of both brands + familiarity, also allows entry into new product category
Mono brands (also "single brands")	Tabasco Huggies Cheer Tide	Strong single brand identity w/o corporate brand, for specific customer need (e.g., P&G and Unilever)

CHAPTER 5

Branding in the B2B World—New Opportunities

Most business people traditionally feel that B2B (business-to-business) is a vastly different world from B2C (business-to-consumer), and their respective business development and marketing practices have nothing in common. This assumption is no longer true. The digital revolution has broadened the scope of resources and tactics used in both worlds and has added intense pressure on B2B marketers to become more customer-focused, competitive, and innovative.

A good example of how social media has affected B2B is illustrated from the recent experience of Patricia Martin, a noted author as well as CEO and founder of LitLamp Communications. She attended the SXSW Interactive conference in Austin, Texas, in March 2012, a huge trade show that serves as "an incubator of cutting-edge technologies." She observed how the incidence and use of social medial had exploded this annual festival in size. In particular, she noted in her March 20, 2012, blog that "B2B brands, especially start-ups, are starting to look more like consumer brands. They have bright, engaging identities and strong brand narratives." Her insight from this experience was that "strong branding of B2B start-ups helps them sell into big and middle market businesses that sign up for the solution, but say 'yes' for the cachet of affiliating with a cool, social media savvy start-up. Furthermore, venture money has been trained to appreciate branding after a decade of betting on consumer focused start-ups." What does this mean? In Patricia's opinion, the opportunity will be that "B2B investors will start to pay for better branding."

Consumer marketing in B2C has long been recognized for its progressive advancements in market research and segmentation, competitive positioning, strategic brand building, innovative marketing practices, and creative thinking. Despite several differences in the marketing and sales dynamics between B2B and B2C, more forward-thinking B2B companies are beginning to discover and adapt many of the basic B2C principles to improve their marketing effectiveness. Here are five opportunity areas for creating more powerful B2B brands and improving marketing efficiencies.

1. Building Strong Customer Loyalty

Any conversation on adapting B2C marketing principles will raise the issue of how the B2B customer is so different. The immediate inference is that sophisticated B2C marketing is not relevant or helpful for any B2B company trying to improve the effectiveness of its marketing team because of this.

The idea that B2C primarily involves mass marketing is no longer true. Our society has become highly fragmented. Media technology and the internet have enabled greater focus, reach, and customization of our marketing efforts to appeal to specific segments in the market, each with different characteristics and needs.

Yet marketing to the typical customer in a B2B situation remains unique in many ways—fewer customers, more complicated decision making, higher, more diverse pricing, greater pressure internally on the buyer to justify his/her purchase decision, longer lead times for the purchase, and greater scrutiny of the product offer. These customer differences sustain the unfortunate, cavalier belief by many that B2B marketing still cannot learn from B2C marketing.

The underlying need to more deeply understand the target customer, especially to achieve a meaningful brand positioning and more innovative marketing initiatives is, in fact, more critical for B2B endeavors, because of the following important differences:

- **More Multileveled Purchasing Decision:** The task of comprehensively examining and approving a purchase in B2B situations is anything but spontaneous. Many people get involved, a variety of different and sometimes conflicting criteria are common, and often an attitude of parochial thinking by the customer (e.g., "only we really understand our business ...") can become an enormous challenge for the B2B marketer (and sales person).

The answer simply requires a more concerted effort to learn everything possible about the customers, who are the people involved in the decision-making process (including the influencers), procedures, and special insights behind the purchase decision, the main business drivers for your customer's success, and importantly how to build a connection of trust and comfort with the buyer.

- **The B2B Company Operates in a More Complex World:** The discipline of segmenting the market to identify and prioritize the ideal target customers can be even more crucial for B2B marketing because it forces one to better understand the customer's needs, issues, and the specific context for decision making in his/ her immediate business category (e.g., who their competition is, how different they are, how/why a product offer can be better customized). This intense evaluation will ultimately facilitate a more constructive dialog with the customer and create a convincing knowledge base that would impress him/her and foster a more respectful, loyal relationship.

- **Offering More than Product Expertise:** Most B2B companies, especially in hi-tech industries, tend to be relentlessly product focused, not brand or customer oriented. Yes, their products (and markets) are more complicated, and so the resulting emphasis is on what these products do. However, not enough attention is focused on what these products or services can do <u>for</u> the customer, and especially how the customer should feel about an offer. In particular, B2B sales people have a tendency to focus only on the features of a product, not the benefits. I recently conducted a "mini ideation workshop" for 75 sales people from a leading paint company, where I emphasized the differences between features and benefits. When the audience described their most creative, relevant new ideas, not one person included what the offer would do <u>for</u> the customer, that is, the benefit. True product differentiation is scant in the B2C world, which forces marketers to rely more on special brand positioning to create a strategic leverage and a high-value perception. The B2B marketers can improve their effectiveness by similarly adding an emotional element to their value proposition, one that is based on customer insights and resonates with the actual user experience.

A good example of a B2B company that has transitioned to a more user-sensitive marketing approach is Microsoft. Long known for its difficult-to-understand, over engineered Windows programs (e.g., Vista), it has since rebounded with a more simplified and personalized brand positioning aimed to build more meaningful relationships with their customers. Their "I'm a PC and Windows 7 was My Idea" campaign reflects this new positioning, which has become the fastest selling operating system in history.

Charles Gold, an experienced tech marketer for over 20 years, recently wrote in an article "Getting Sophisticated: What B2B Tech Marketers Must Learn from B2C"[1] that tech marketers are relatively unsophisticated and rely on blunt instruments, not precision tools. A key driver for this essential transition is the emergence of the younger "Z" Generation that has grown up with expectations about products based on "elegant user experiences"—plain spoken communications and pervasive social networks. And these younger, savvy, and demanding people will also be tomorrow's B2B customer.

Marketing for both B2B and B2C should always start with the target customer, but there is still ample room for improvement in the B2B world by studying and adapting other approaches to strengthen customer loyalty.

2. A More Compelling Value Proposition

Another opportunity for B2B marketers to learn from B2C practices is researching and improving their "Value Proposition." This concept has always been a predominant strategic tool for marketing in B2C categories, and is now becoming more ubiquitous in B2B industries. What has driven the importance of this principle recently is the recession and how customers today view and judge "good value." Their biggest concern for the future lies overwhelmingly in the economy. This macroeconomic reality is impacting the behavior of all decision makers, in two critical ways: (1) a reduction in consumption in many categories (e.g., entertainment), delay of major purchases (e.g., home improvements), and/or resorting to cheaper products; and (2) for more essential goods and services, people will trade down to stretch their money, demonstrating higher price sensitivity and decreased usage.

Everyone is simply more sensitive to what they will be getting for their money or the price they pay. The underlying concept of "value" in this context of a value proposition is based on a basic formula:

$$Value = \frac{Benefit}{Price}$$

The term "proposition" implies a promise of value, or what can be offered and delivered to the customer to enhance the product/company brand equity (e.g., essentially the perceived value of the brand) and customer loyalty. While there are many definitions of "value proposition," the one I prefer is more customer driven and very appropriate for B2B companies:

> *It is a clear statement about the tangible business results customers can get from using your product, service or solution. Busy decision-makers don't care about what you're selling. They only care about what it does for them.*[2]

In other words, a value proposition defines the primary reason why a customer or prospect should buy from you and not the competition. A company must find a relevant and credible way to differentiate its offer from competitors, and ideally identify at least one key element of value where they need to excel. This is the ultimate challenge for any brand positioning.

Importance of Being Customer Focused

A good value proposition must be customer driven, not based solely on a product's attributes. In his book *Building Strong Brands*,[3] David Aaker refers to the "Product-Attribute Fixation Trap," in which the strategic and tactical management of a brand is focused on product attributes. The assumption here is that these attributes are the only relevant bases for customer decisions and competitive dynamics.

This is a common challenge for technology companies in particular that are obsessed with the intricacies of the product's functional performance. The key is to focus more on the reasons why your customer could use your offering, or what they really care about when making decisions. Understanding the formulaic definition of value will help. A concerted effort to diligently research customers will help identify new insights and ways to enhance the perceived benefit or solution. This will enable B2B marketers to then establish an optimal price that will accurately reflect the relevance and importance of the perceived quality of this benefit.

What to Ask Yourself (and Customers) to Identify Opportunities for Improvement

When developing the value proposition to maximize the perceived value of your offering, here are some useful questions that we ask B2B clients internally and/or customers in research:

- Why do people buy from our company in the first place? What value do they seek? Expect? Hope for?
- What are we doing to meet their expectations? What are we not doing?
- What are the customer's true "pain points" or problems?
- What is our "niche/specialization" or area of excellence? Do customers recognize this?
- How do customers actually think and talk about our business? What must they be convinced of to start buying from my company?
- What can I change or add to my value proposition to cause my customers to say, "I would have to be crazy to do business with someone else?"

How to Overcome Typical Pricing Issues to Enhance Your Value Proposition

Solutions must begin with smart research that diagnoses the reasons behind frequent customer complaints, especially those threats that can adversely impact the balance between the perceived benefit and the price. Following are the examples of common problems and possible solutions:

1. "The superior benefit is not worth the price premium"
   a. Add or enhance an emotional element to the end benefit
   b. Leverage the price as a signal of quality
   c. Create new copy to elevate the perceived worth

2. "I already have the same benefit with my cheaper choice"
   a. Question the cheaper option to shake the customer's complacency
   b. Focus on your superiority, perhaps with a credible endorsement
   c. Offer an extra reason to support the benefit and to buy it

3. "I can't afford it, it is way too expensive for me"
   a. Reframe the absolute price (e.g., change the unit of measure or perceived price point)
   b. Emphasize any side savings
   c. Highlight the risks of not buying it

4. "Sure it's cheap, but I doubt the quality"
   a. Reassure the customer on the quality (e.g., leverage product strengths, brand history, or special ingredients/components)
   b. Use others to sell the quality (e.g., a spokesperson who epitomizes value, or how everyone else thinks it's high quality)

Creating a relevant and credible value proposition will be meaningful only if it is consistently used to guide all marketing and sales initiatives, from phone calls, emails, voice mails to advertising and actual presentations to customers. The concept of optimizing value is too important for your success to treat lightly when defining the ideal value proposition. I suggest you address three fundamental questions (and typical answers), which will help you determine whether your current value proposition needs improvement:

1. Have the market conditions, including competition, changed enough during the past 3 years so that your value proposition warrants a new review?
   a. Yes, so you should consider whether/how to strengthen it
   b. Not sure, but it makes sense to re-assess these market dynamics to validate it
   c. No, I am positive my value proposition is still solid and relevant (if this is your answer, there may be a risk in this assumption)

2. Do your primary customers recognize, appreciate, and are still motivated by the promise in your value proposition?
   a. Yes, because we get feedback from them all the time that confirms its viability
   b. Not sure, because we don't spend enough time or resources getting objective, comprehensive feedback
   c. No, doubt it, because we have been getting mixed signals and more pressure on our pricing from them

3. Do your marketing and sales teams consistently and convincingly communicate the same message, based on your current value proposition?

    a. Yes, at least that is what my senior managers convey to me

    b. Not sure, as we don't always monitor their messages carefully

    c. No, don't think so because the coordination and communications between our marketing and sales personnel can be improved

3. How Value Pricing Can Prevent Perceptions of "Commoditization"

The digital revolution has transformed business models in many ways, especially this preoccupation of "best value," and related to this is the ease for anyone comparing prices online for similar products or services. A recent survey by IBM[4] among 1,730 CMOs around the world underscored the perplexing effects of accessible data on this search for "best value." The survey results show that the biggest challenges CMOs face today are driven by this new digital age:

1. Data explosion (71%)
2. Social media (68%)
3. Growth of channel and device choices (65%)

    With the internet, people can easily learn more about the cost of any product or service these days. An increasingly common challenge for B2B companies is to combat the tendency of buyers from applying intense pressure to lower their prices. It is basically a fight against "commoditization." When there is little convincing difference from competition (i.e., including a perception of lower quality), purchasers will exert their influence to drive this commoditization. After all, squeezing down the price is often how they are judged and rewarded, and the only rational way to differentiate commodities is the price, which favors the buyer, not the seller. And often the purchaser has a good idea of the seller's cost these days.

    The full impact of this data explosion has even affected sales at retail. A recent article in *The New York* Times, "Knowing Cost, the Customer

Sets the Price,"[5] described how the shopper can today haggle down prices due to the internet and shopping comparison apps. If the retailer balks, some shoppers will walk, going to Amazon and eBay instead.

How to Fight Commoditization with Value Pricing

B2B marketers can learn a lot from B2C on how to enhance the perceived value of their products or services. Instead of being overly focused on product details and capabilities, as so many B2B marketers and sales people are, they should become more customer focused and learn what more can be done to satisfy their needs, even delight them. The insights from a more intense scrutiny of the customer will become the basis for more creative, prudent, and relevant value pricing.

Wikipedia defines value pricing (or really "value-based pricing") as a "business strategy that sets prices primarily on the perceived value to the customer, rather than on the actual cost of the product, the market price, competitor's prices, or the historical price."[6] In both B2C and B2B, the perception of value is based on how the customer views the benefit or solution offered—its quality, worthiness, distinctiveness, and relevance to the customer's needs, plus how they feel emotionally about it. The goal of value pricing should be to align the price with this perceived value (i.e., the benefit, ideally with an indication of the quantitative measurement of its impact) promised and delivered to the customer.

This IBM survey also found that the most proactive CMOs are responding to these digital challenges by trying to understand the customers as individuals, not as markets. They are focusing on relationships (the basis for successful branding), not transactions. This includes a commitment to developing a more clear "corporate brand character" as well.

The vast majority of CMOs in this survey identified three key areas for improvement, which will all help marketers and sales people fight this problem of commoditization:

1. **Deliver Value to Empowered Customers:** B2B marketers must not only learn what customers need or want, but also identify individual insights on what they value most and how they behave. This will be accomplished by going beyond traditional research, too.

Approximately 80% of the CMOs said they plan to use customer analytics, CRM or customer relationship management, social media, and mobile apps more extensively to identify these underlying insights and "hidden wishes."

2. **Foster Lasting Connections:** In today's age of digital technology, it is easy for customers to learn about the seller and competitive offers, and then go elsewhere. This is why a top priority is to cultivate strong customer loyalty. In B2B, this includes building the corporate character or brand image, for both external customers and internal employees, and across all touch points and experiences. Today, what an organization stands for is as important as what it sells. Approximately 75% of these CMOs believe marketing must manage brand reputation within and beyond the enterprise.

3. **Capture Value, Measure Results:** There is increasing pressure to justify marketing expenditures and maximize the return on marketing investment. A disconcerting trend, especially in B2B circles, is a disproportionate emphasis on selling tactics and using data to manage the transaction, not on sustaining the relationship with the customer. Of the four Ps (promotion, products, place, and price), CMOs feel they should play a greater role shaping the latter three Ps. This will help marketers develop more meaningful, customized programs, offers, and special services to enhance the perception of the "benefit/solution" promised, and thus improve their value pricing effectiveness.

Customers will continue to become more proficient in learning about a seller's costs and competitive alternatives. The real challenge for B2B marketers is to improve their research to better understand individual buyers' value desires and behavior, to be more innovative by creating new ideas for a better offer, and to allocate more resources for managing their relationship with buyers going forward.

4. Marketing and Sales Alignment—Breaking Down Silos

The phenomenon of silo mentality has become a major problem today. In many companies it causes a dangerous disconnect between marketing and sales, especially in B2B where the sales role has traditionally predominated (marketing is more proactive in B2C companies, and so the problem is not usually severe). The result is lost opportunities and revenues, increased market entry costs, longer sales cycles, wasted marketing materials, and overall higher cost of sales. Consider the following alarming signs of inefficiencies:

- Approximately 80% of marketing leads in B2B are lost or ignored by sales today
- Approximately 70% of marketing collateral is never used by sales
- Most ignored leads are for the long term, which can represent 77% of potential company revenues

Source: Marketing Sherpa

Both sales and marketing end up pointing blameful fingers at each other. Silos may exist in other functional departments too (e.g., PR, HR, IT Operations), but this lack of integration or alignment between sales and marketing is probably the most ubiquitous issue that is haunting many CEOs today. Years ago, Peter Drucker said "Sales and marketing functions can never align; they are opposing functions, not parallel ones." However, business has changed dramatically since then. Technological advancements, more aggressive competition, tighter budgets, and intensifying pressure to measure performance have forced CEOs to finally acknowledge these inefficiencies and to develop new solutions.

One of the problems leading to this silo mentality is that the roles of marketing and sales have become blurred in many B2B companies. An executive at a major health care company recently said that most of their marketing services are outsourced now, including traditional strategic initiatives such as brand positioning, business plan development, all public relations, creative input for packaging and advertising, competitive analyses, and most promotional initiatives. At the same time, sales has expanded its functions to control almost every other aspect of traditional marketing and customer servicing.

There are several drivers behind this emergence of silo behavior. One of the most important causes is the recent recession and the pressures on achieving key business results. Tightening one's belt has forced marketing to become more careful about budgeting and justifying all initiatives, including measuring the outcome, which has created intense pressure for procuring enough funds and defending their actions. By contrast, declining demand has made it very difficult for sales to find new buyers, and so their focus is more on controlling interaction with their current customers.

Another key factor is the explosion of digital access and social media platforms. This offers marketing new low-cost opportunities to interact directly with customers and track their success, even converting identified leads to customers (generally a sales function). Meanwhile, sales is using these digital vehicles to gain more insights on the customer's buying behavior and a better understanding of the influencer network (i.e., usually the domain of marketing).

These merging roles beg the question of what should be the responsibilities and expectations for both the marketing and sales roles today. Traditionally, the role of marketing has been more strategic, while sales is more tactical—marketing generates the demand and leads, and sales closes the deal. Marketing people care about the brand. Sales people care about the deal.

One of the key sources of these conflicts is that the brand value proposition and rationale are not translated down to sales in a practical, specific, or actionable way. People in sales get frustrated when marketing provides them with too much communication about the brand, but it is not broken down into tactical arguments, selling points, or concise programs. As a result, sales people often view marketing people in an "ivory tower" way. Sales people have very little time in front of clients and prospects. A 5-minute presentation on the brand will take a back seat to more immediate pitches on the price and key features of the product. In short, the brand messages should be customized to fit the realities of the sales world. If not, those pretty brand brochures will continue to collect dust.

How to Eliminate These Silos

The first task for senior management is to recognize this phenomenon and the causes behind it, especially how the roles of each may have merged. Then here are some specific steps that would help integrate the marketing and sales functions to minimize overlap and more effectively grow a business:

1. **Make it a Top Priority—with Bite:** Senior management should re-structure these roles with new job descriptions, special bonuses for achieving a more productive alignment, and create an ongoing mechanism for more open, frequent discussions between marketing and sales. Ideally, both marketing and sales should report to one director or EVP. In addition, a staff person reporting to this head should be responsible for all sales and marketing communications.

2. **Create a Special "Integration Team":** Assign one key person from marketing and sales (plus other disciplines, as necessary, such as HR, IT) to establish common business goals, break down the silos, and conduct meetings at least every other week to discuss upcoming activities and review the dashboard that everyone reports into, and also to frequently report the progress to senior leadership.

3. **Initiate "Change Management":** The process of generating and converting leads is crucial and it must be clearly spelled out who does what between marketing and sales. This may require extreme measures to ensure the follow-up details are well coordinated and monitored by senior management. The CEO must create a new environment where common goals are understood and achieved as a team.

Eliminating this silo mentality will require a concerted, ongoing effort as it will involve some fundamental cultural changes. People must no longer treat marketing and sales as departments but as groups of individuals, motivating each person with high potential to contribute toward a common goal of creating added value for the customer. Ideally, marketing should take the time to see how the sales team operates on a daily basis so that they can make selling easier, more efficient, and more effective. Sometimes bringing in outside, neutral expertise can help bridge this gap. Global Partners, a consulting and training firm from Cambridge, Massachusetts, focuses on B2B issues like this.

5. Why Emotion Is Critical for B2B Brand Marketing

Another subtle yet crucial opportunity involves adding emotion to a company's marketing and sales approach. While B2B must improve its ability to enhance the perceived value of its offers, how to incorporate a relevant emotional dynamic in its brand positioning and initiatives may be the most challenging for many traditional B2B marketers.

There are many noteworthy differences between B2B and B2C marketing that help explain why the B2B approach is traditionally more rational—for example, with longer sales cycles, more complex, fewer buyers, price variations for different buyers or situations, purchasing prospects conducting more research, more people involved in the decision process, personal interactions being more important, and greater influence by third parties. The typical B2B process starts with an explanation of *what* the product or service offers, then *how* it works, and finally *why* it makes sense for the prospect and his/her company. It is the classic what–how–why approach, with the hope that ultimately this process will engender a sense of trust with the buyer. The emphasis is always on a rational, formulaic evaluation, with little or no emotion included, even though building one-to-one personal relationships is more common, pronounced, and critical in B2B.

Meanwhile, the intense competitive nature and the sophistication of branding in the B2C world has elevated marketing beyond the rational and forced a greater emotional involvement. Brand marketing is all about building a trustful relationship with a customer. Much of B2C advertising is impulse or experience oriented, frequently designed to convince customers to "want" something, rather than pandering to a "need" for a product that is more likely in B2B. Apple is a great example. No one "needed" an iPad or iPhone until Apple created a contagious, passionate desire for these new products, contributed by the customer's ubiquitous emotional love for Apple, cultivated over time. In addition, the Apple brand became very "cool" and people simply wanted that emotional "halo" and image to extend to themselves.

The Growing Importance of "Brand Trust"

There is no emotional driver more important for building a sustained relationship with target customers than the feeling of trust. So many variables are at play for determining the trust for a brand—confidence, integrity, reliability, credibility, the level of certainty, etc. The annual Edelman Trust Index survey shows that the level of trust for brands and business leaders has declined significantly in recent years. While the economic and pricing values for B2B decision making will always be vital, the increasing complexity of their buying process has caused the subjective value of trust to become even more crucial.

This growing lack of trust is particularly evident among the emerging millennial segment (those born after 1980). A recent survey of 400 millennials by a marketing consulting firm, Social Chorus, showed a serious distrust level for brand advertising—only 6% consider online advertising to be credible (probably worse for traditional advertising), whereas feedback from their peers is the most influential for their purchase decisions (95% say their friends are the most credible source of information). A sense of trust for this emerging powerhouse group is essential: 92% say "trust" plays a key role on who influences them online.

Another area where brand trust is becoming more critical is cross-cultural relationships. Every foreign market has different business practices and a unique culture, so it is natural to be suspicious and distrustful of any new venture from the outside. Companies must recognize these barriers, and working with local managers, conduct insightful research to better understand their special emotional drivers and create new ideas for relevant marketing initiatives that would appeal to their cultural passions.

The intangible value of a brand trust and/or a company reputation is a significant contributor of a company's valuation as well. Other sources of intangible value are a company or brand's market position, its business systems (proprietary software, processes, etc.) and its knowledge (R&D, patents, human capital, etc.). In their book *The Brand Bubble*, John Gerzema and Edward Lebar estimate that in the 1950s about 30% of a firm's value was intangible. Today, it is closer to 62% globally.

Creating value is no longer just about the quality of a product or service. Today, it is also about the quality of a company's conduct, both internally and externally. There is greater transparency with the internet these days, so any trust deficit will act as a deterrent to a firm's long-term growth. Six of the world's top ten brands from Interbrand's global surveys are technology companies: Apple, IBM, Microsoft, Google, Intel, and HP. Something they all have in common is the unprecedented amount of personal data that is entrusted to them. As a result, they are committed to forging deep emotional connections with consumers, especially trust.

Trust and brand leadership are a function of the many quiet decisions and judgment calls that a company's management makes about its own values. In a 2011 article "Why Trust Matters More Than Ever for Brands" in the *Harvard Business Review*, Deepa Prahalad offers some helpful examples of how reputable companies have taken the initiative to secure this sense of trust in their corporate brand: "Apple saying that it will not accept apps for pornography, SC Johnson going beyond the industry standard to be more transparent about the ingredients in its products, the Tata Group retaining every single employee and hotel contractor after the 2008 Mumbai attacks."

Brand trust is also essential in B2C, especially with the explosion of social media marketing. Mark Fidelman, CEO for Evolve, an influencer engagement and marketing consulting firm, alluded to the results of their recent survey to reinforce the importance of trust: 73% of consumers base their buying decision on "trust", more than any other emotion. The key ingredients for developing a healthy level of trust include credibility, reliability, and intimacy (i.e., comfort in a brand).

According to Fidelman, every consumer naturally has their own "community of trust," consisting primarily of family and friends. In addition, the internet has created such an extensive interactive communication network that has allowed for trustworthy, independent "influencers" and "brand advocates" to emerge in various categories. They have also become credible members of this community of trust and can play a significant role in word-of-mouth sharing or marketing. Using the simple "AIDA" model, influencers have an impact on the "awareness" and "interest" phases, whereas advocates are most convincing for encouraging the "desire" and "action" for buying decisions. Mark Fidelman underscores the importance of identifying and working with such brand influencers and advocates building a sense of trust for such purchases and enhancing brand loyalty over the long run.

Creating a more trustful relationship is not easy, but developing a relevant and appealing brand persona is essential. Whether it involves an idealistic emerging segment like millennials, or an increasingly complicated decision-making process in B2B, or a dynamic, transformative category like healthcare, the brand content must include new, meaningful trust-building ideas. The rise of "purposeful branding" reflects a trend that is becoming more prevalent, especially for millennials. The Social Chorus survey indicated that millennials strongly favor credible content that embraces new social responsibility and environmental deeds. Internationally, the growing visibility and active response to indigenous corruption in many parts of the world (e.g., Brazil, China, India, Russia, plus the worldwide financial and banking industry) is making this notion of brand trust even more important.

Related to this, Erich Joachimsthaler, founder and CEO of Vivaldi Partners, recently inaugurated a survey among 1000 business leaders on the perceived value and health of over 60 brands. The results determined a new value ranking for each, a "Brand Social Currency" score, another indication of the "brand trust" for these companies. Among the most trusted brands were JetBlue, Virgin, and Southwest in the airline category, Starbucks in the fast food area, and not surprisingly, Apple.

How to Add Emotions in B2B Marketing

The opportunity to make the "why" argument so much more convincing with relevant emotions is compelling. In B2B, human relationships are more personally interactive and important, and so emotions such as trust, confidence, fear avoidance, and caring are powerful ingredients for cultivating a stronger relationship. In his classic instructional video, Simon Sinek talks about "How Great Leaders Inspire Action,"[7] and how the "why" you believe is more important than the "what" you do. Sinek uses Apple, The Wright Brothers, and Martin Luther King to demonstrate powerful emotions such as believing and loyalty.

Here are some specific steps that can enhance the value of a B2B proposition, through the addition of an emotional link to marketing initiatives:

- **Customer Research:** More diligent research on the client and his/her main purchase drivers, including emotional motivations, will provide insights on new ways to connect and nurture more trust.
- **Company Brand:** In B2B, the individual product or service brands are not nearly as important as the corporate brand equity, so this must contain relevant, emotional promises. Although practical purchase criteria usually drive product selection (e.g., performance, capabilities, price), the ultimate value of the parent brand perceived

by buyers will complete the purchase decision—Can I believe in this company? Can I trust them? Will they deliver on their promises?

- **Storytelling:** Perhaps the most powerful tool for building confidence and a loyal relationship is to tell a personal story that reiterates key values and emotional benefits. These should reflect the corporate brand and be used in websites, advertising, promotional material, sales pitches, etc., ideally based on insights identified in customer research to ensure they are relevant to the buyer as well. The importance of storytelling was emphasized by Chip and Dan Heath who recently wrote about content and communications in their book *Made to Stick*. This excellent book elaborated on the concept of "stickiness," which was popularized by Malcolm Gladwell in his noteworthy book *The Tipping Point*. The Heath brothers summarized what can make content and communications "sticky" or successful using six principles captured in the acronym "SUCCES":
  - **"S" Simplicity:** Stripping an idea to its <u>core</u>, prioritizing, creating ideas that are simple and profound (using proverbs), focusing (people don't remember lists of ideas)
  - **"U" Unexpectedness:** Use <u>surprise</u> to grab people's attention, generate interest, and engage curiosity
  - **"C" Concreteness:** To make our ideas <u>clear</u>, relate to human actions and concrete images, emphasize the substance and relevance, and avoid the abstract
  - **"C" Credibility:** To make people <u>believe</u> and agree with ideas, help people test ideas for themselves, and use hard numbers to build a case to be remembered
  - **"E" Emotions:** How to <u>care</u> about ideas—we're wired to feel things for people, so don't use vague abstractions
  - **"S" Stories:** To get people to <u>act</u> on ideas and identify with them, preparing them to respond more effectively. Well-crafted stories inspire emotions that lead to decision making
- **Social Media:** Peer feedback and recommendations through these new interactive media options have a greater impact on purchase decisions today. It also offers an ideal way for vendors to build their one-to-one customer relationships, assuming the emotional promises are aligned with the corporate brand.

CHAPTER 6

Marketing Today: Branding for Digital Marketing and Social Media

Transformative Shifts in the Marketplace, Consumer Tastes and Media

The goal of branding is to form an emotional, loyal relationship with the target customer. Engaging your customer is critical for this goal, and the internet today presents extraordinary opportunities to start a conversation with target customers due to its interactive capabilities.

Since World War II, we have been living in a world of mega brands like Tide, Coca-Cola, and Crest, which were designed to appeal to a mass market. In the past decade, this world had changed dramatically. Mass marketing has evolved into micro marketing. This fundamental change reflects both the nature of the marketplace as well as new opportunities to cost efficiently reach specific segments of the market.

Years ago, consumers wanted to belong and keep up with the crowd. Today they want to stand out from the crowd. American society is far more diverse and commercially self-indulgent. It has splintered into countless market segments defined not only by demography (e.g., Hispanic, Asian, Gay, etc.), but also by product preferences driven by a feeling that "it is so right for me". At the same time, the clutter is immense and still growing. There are over 2 million products in supermarkets today, with more than 700 new introductions each day. In retail outlets, scanning equipment is constantly providing marketers with tons of personal data on consumers' attitudes, desires, habits and purchase preferences.

Concurrent with this accelerating fragmentation and expanding overload of product options, the changes in the media vehicles for reaching our target audience are just as significant. In the 1960's an advertiser could reach 80% of U.S. women with one spot aired simultaneously on CBS, NBC and ABC. Today an ad would have to run on 100 TV channels to get even close to this target. The big change is in the spread of digital and wireless communication channels, consisting of focused cable TV and radio channels, specialized magazines, and millions of computer terminals, video-game consoles, personal digital assistants and cell-phone screens. The use of media has become far more targeted to reach these special interest segments and to form new brand relationships with consumers:

- Households received 27 TV channels in 1994, today over 200 TV Channels
- Share of prime time: cable—52% , broadcast—44%
- All *new* magazine introductions are "specialty" oriented and targeted
- Total ad revenue for mass media is growing 3.5% per year, for micro media,13.5% per year

How the Internet Has Changed the Way Consumers Buy

Perhaps the most revolutionary change involves the purchasing habits of consumers. Trust is crucial. According to ACNielsen, 85% of consumers trust the recommendation of another person, whereas only 14% of people generally trust traditional advertising. In light of these trends, you can appreciate more the power of word-of-mouth (WOM) marketing for finding and leveraging credible sources of information. Product areas that are natural fits for WOM include the entertainment and electronics industries, do-it-yourself projects, food, beverages, packaged goods, and home products.

Internet engagement is especially pronounced among high-potential purchasers. Educating oneself for such purchases online has become pervasive, with many high-powered consumers religiously following social platforms such as blogs, websites, and specific product forums that discuss all relevant details of a product category. According to research from BlogHer and Compass Partners, 35% of women aged 18 to 75 participate in the blogosphere weekly, 53% of women read online blogs, 37% post comments, and 28% write or update blogs. Another important consumer group is the millennials, a market segment (born after 1980) of 79 million people with projected spending power of $170 billion in the next 5 years. Of these millennials, 91% say they will buy a product based on a friend's recommendation. Also, studies by comScore, ACNielsen, and Harris Interactive show how dominant the internet has become for influencing these purchase habits:

- 90% of all purchase decisions begin on the internet.
- 75% of people shop online before they buy offline.
- 85% are looking for an independent review.

The Rise of "Content Marketing"

My experience with most of my students at NYU in their 20s and 30s is that they are so much more interested and skilled than I am in social media and other forms of digital communications (especially mobile), but they severely lack a genuine understanding of the importance of the message itself. This is why I constantly emphasize that branding is so critical for success—if researched and developed properly, it will help you create content that is compelling, relevant, credible, and distinctive.

The Content Marketing Institute defines *content marketing* as a "marketing technique of creating and distributing relevant and valuable content to attract, acquire, and engage a clearly defined target audience." Much of the content is education-based, so naturally it is becoming very common in B2B circles as well. The most pervasive communication vehicle for content marketing is social media (79%), yet paradoxically it is also perceived to be the least effective (69%) of all platforms (Source: 10/10 compendium survey from the Content Marketing Institute). The main reason for this apparent contradiction is that there is a general lack of confidence in social media for this purpose, since research experts don't know yet how to effectively measure social media and its impact on brands.

The biggest challenge for marketers is producing engaging content (36%), followed by producing enough content (21%). Another key issue is how to protect brand integrity, as 40% feel that social media creates special challenges for this important task.

The use of social media for branding is still in an embryonic stage of proven, quantified effectiveness, despite the enormous potential for reaching and engaging customers. Like so many challenges rising from our new online world, plus the upheaval of traditional business principles from the recent recession, the attributes of creativity and innovation will be the most important weapons for marketers in the future. For example, there is statistical evidence proving that the "creative" element of new content is four to five times more important than the communication vehicle itself (e.g., a social medium like Facebook) (Source: "Insight Express" research firm).

In November 2011, David Dunn wrote an article on "30 Ways to Make It Easier for Your Customers to Buy," which provided helpful tips on how to market content. He points out how internet technology has dramatically increased the number and efficiency for producing and then delivering content formats. David refers to six pillars or types of marketing, the main benefit and common ways to market content for each:

- Traditional (Awareness)
  - Magazines and newspapers
  - Press releases on availability, submit to newswires, etc.
  - Mail content to clients and key prospects
  - Handouts at events (e.g., trade shows)
  - Add to corporate press/information packets
  - Comarket with other brands
- Content (Education)
  - Cross-link and reference various content marketing formats, as appropriate
- Web (Interaction)
  - Place content on website in various locations
  - Optimize metatags for search engines
  - Offer webinars to promote white papers, booklets, e-books
  - Employ keyword advertising on search engine sites
  - Banner ads to drive traffic to website
  - Submit to websites that specialize in distributing articles
  - Buy and send to a third-party email list
  - Put link to your content in your email signature block
  - Add content to an online press kit

- o Translate content into a podcast
- o Submit to online syndications services
- Social (Conversation)
  - o Set up Facebook page for your content
  - o Post availability on your blog and Twitter accounts
  - o Invite readers to forward to a friend
  - o Convert/adapt content to video version (e.g., YouTube)
  - o Make content available through RSS
  - o Forward to bookmarking sites (e.g., Digg)
  - o Mention in online communities
- Mobile (Convenience)
  - o Develop app for content download from the web
  - o Adapt content for e-readers and smart phones
- Personal (Peer-to-Peer)
  - o Present at speaking engagements—slides, white papers as leave-behinds
  - o Use WOM marketing
  - o Get on business radio to discuss your content
  - o Get testimonials to promote your content (e.g., for LinkedIn)
  - o List web URL of content media on your business card

Importance of Integrated Marketing

Despite our obsession with digital marketing, the use of traditional marketing and communication vehicles has not disappeared. One theory is that online communications lacks strong emotional or experiential impact, especially compared to a vehicle like television. It is called the "Lean Back" versus the "Lean Forward" argument. Proponents of traditional advertising (e.g., TV) argue that this medium offers entertainment, which makes one "lean back" to enjoy, so the interruption of commercials essentially jolts the mind with more impact. Hence the "passive" consuming medium of TV can stir up emotions more easily in the limbic part of the brain, which is the main receptor of emotions.

Meanwhile the main use of the internet is to get information or contacts, thus stimulating one's attention level so much that he or she "leans forward." As a result of this focus, any advertising appearing alongside the core content is often viewed as an annoyance, that is, the preoccupying content drowns out the ad impact. These online ads therefore rarely impact the limbic system, but instead remain as "cognitive cortex" thoughts that lack emotional resonance.

The conclusion from this theory is that it is best to use a combination of traditional and online advertising, or "integrated advertising." Both used prudently with the right target consumers can enhance the emotional appeal of brands while also creating a buzz and sharing relevant brand messages or content.

How the Role of "Marketing" Is Changing in Corporations

In light of these seismic transformations caused mainly by the internet, the role of the marketer in most progressive companies is becoming broader and more visionary. One noteworthy change is the blurring of the marketing and sales responsibilities, especially in B2B industries. The task of learning even more about the customer and how to fully engage him or her is becoming more important and will be the key for defining the future role of marketing. Here are five critical opportunities that will help marketers become more visionary and influential in this new world of social media:

1. Today's marketer must go beyond developing the marketing plan and focus more on the key drivers for a broader business strategy. Becoming the master of customer insights will be vital, as this will enhance his or her trust and credibility within an organization.

2. Recognize that brand building will be different. It used to involve primarily controlling the brand message, but now it must emphasize engaging customers online, encouraging transparent conversations, creating content that offers genuine value, and inspiring sharing with friends.

3. Initiate innovation. Instead of emphasizing incremental improvements, focus on innovative strategies and actions that optimize customer experiences, alternative distribution channels, new pricing policies and transformative business models.

4. Redefine and practice a new version of "marketing excellence." This should build on traditional marketing communications, and embrace all levers of digital marketing (and sales) that will maximize the added value derived from marketing investments.

5. Create a broader innovative culture that is more customer centric, developing new ways to enhance customer experiences and drive growth.

Impact on Branding

Given this rifle shot approach to marketing (e.g., figuring out the right way to send the right message to the right person), what does it mean for branding? Basically the ground rules for brand development don't change so much as the degree of thoroughness and creativity that will be required to make brands stand out and cut through the clutter. Here are the major implications for brand marketing in the future:

- A greater challenge for accurately defining each target customer segment and more fully understanding the market potential, the demographics and all subtle nuances of their emotional needs and usage habits.
- Strong brands will become even more important for penetrating the clutter, differentiating from competition, and building loyal customer relationships.
- At the same time, an emergence of niche brands, product extensions and mass customization will lead to an abundance of new variations
- Marketing productivity should improve for the savvy marketer. P&G spent 10% of its sales on advertising five years ago, and achieved a 4% bump in sales, whereas last year this same ad/sales level generated a 9% increase in unit volume.
- The emotions for brand selection and product use will become even more vital for building a strong brand personality, sustaining a competitive advantage and nurturing consumer loyalty.
- Positioning a brand to be compelling and truly relevant, and also customizing the marketing to send a personalized message (and product) to each user, must become more sophisticated

- Good brand marketing will require more creativity to engage the customer in each market segment.
- The biggest difference between this new digital marketing and traditional marketing is that the former is interactive, and the brand manager is no longer in control of his/her brand. Hence integrity, transparency, and credibility are crucial for successful branding today.
- Managing a brand, especially with integrated marketing programs (e.g., both traditional and digital) is today more complicated, yet more critical since the power of online communications is more in the hands of the consumer.

Five Issues to Determine Whether/How to Market Your Brand in Social Media

1. *Target Customer*—who and what is most relevant for your target, and can you offer a meaningful value proposition via social media?
2. *Point of Difference*—the permission to talk and engage will depend on the credibility and trust of the brand benefit and its support features.
3. *Brand Personality*—all content and use of social media should be consistent with the brand personality. People will want to engage with a brand if they view it more like a human being, especially with an appealing emotional dimension.
4. *Relevant Message*—smart research will be essential to identify customer insights that will ensure development of a distinctive creative hook, to offer enough value and newsworthiness so people will want to talk and share.
5. *Defining Success*—quantitative measurements of ROI must reflect all marketing initiatives, traditional and digital, and relate to key business goals.

Conclusion: 20 Key Principles for Developing Strong Brands

1. **Branding Is a Tool:** Everyone wants to believe they have the ideal brand. It's not an "end-all" situation. A brand is a tool to build

consumer loyalty and brand equity. Branding is more than a name or logo. It is a core message and impression—what you want a product (or service, corporation, country, university, or even yourself) to mean to your customer, something special and valuable.

2. **The Customer Is the "Authority," Not You:** Work hard and you may feel like an expert, but you'll always be surprised; what the consumer tells you is more important than what you think you know about a brand.

3. **Perceptions Are Reality:** How the consumer views your brand and the competition is what counts, more than what the apparent "facts" indicate. You are competing for a share of your customer's mind.

4. **Start with the Market Opportunity:** Begin any expansion effort with an analysis of the marketplace, to understand how consumers perceive their own problems/needs, and the competition in a category, and to identify new opportunities for brand positioning and future growth.

5. **Competition Changes, So Must You:** We live in a dynamic world in which competition is constantly trying to take business away from you with new promises or claims. You must stay one step ahead by constantly talking to consumers and monitoring your competition.

6. **Consumer Insights Are the Best Source for Ideas:** Start with the consumer, be creative, develop hypotheses, and go back to the consumer again and again for feedback, until you discover that elusive insight that will enable you to touch that critical "hot button" and distinguish your brand.

7. **Positioning Makes You Focus:** A diligent consumer research and creative ideation can help you identify and focus on the two essential elements of the positioning statement: How to meaningfully address a consumer need and be different from competition.

8. **You're Not There Until You Have an Emotional Brand:** It's not just what you can do for the customer (added value or the "benefit"), but also how you make him/her feel that will determine your success.

9. **Positioning Can Change, but Not the Brand Essence:** To remain relevant to consumers and different from competition, elements of a brand positioning may be refined (carefully), but the core essence of the brand is its soul and should rarely change, if prudently developed and defined.

10. **A Brand Must Add Value to Capture Consumers' Interest:** With competition intensifying in almost every category, the challenge is to maximize the brand value as viewed by consumers, a function of the perceived benefit and pricing. Good creativity is essential for this.

11. **Work Doesn't Stop When You Finally Define Your Brand:** The world is not static, so just when you think you have finally developed (and tested) the ideal positioning and brand identity, you must then manage the brand creatively and proactively to strengthen its brand equity and to keep up with competition and evolving consumer dynamics.

12. **Brand Equity Doesn't Just "Happen":** Another term often misused and/or improperly measured. Actually, brand equity simply represents how your customer values your brand. It takes a long time and smart, consistent marketing to cultivate a strong emotional connection with the customer, which is the essence of brand equity.

13. **Strong Brand Equity Offers Many Advantages:** It allows for premium pricing, higher profits, economies in spending, customer loyalty, and a platform for brand expansion, but not without risks of undermining the integrity of the core brand when the link to the brand heritage is questionable.

14. **Umbrella Branding Is Not So Easy:** A strong brand identity doesn't necessarily open doors to new market segments or target customers, but it can enhance the credibility (reason-to-believe) and emotional attachment for a sub-brand or brand extension, if properly positioned.

15. **A Brand Is the Emotional Compass for Growth:** The power of a good brand is the direction it provides, by leveraging the same emotions for new extensions, new uses, new customers, and new marketing practices.

16. **Consider All Possible "Weapons" to Distinguish Your Brand:** Start with the brand name and packaging design, the basis for all immediate (and lasting) impressions, plus the possible added value of the corporate name for separating your brand from the pack.

17. **Advertising Is Execution, Not Branding:** Work with ad agencies and other creative suppliers, but developing the brand message is the first and most critical step, a strategic responsibility that should not be delegated.

18. **Think of a Brand as a Person:** Branding is about emotional relationships with a human, not a thing, so the best way to create a captivating brand is to describe it like a person, often mirroring the profile/ personality of your heavy or ideal customer, which will also help guide all creative efforts to communicate and establish the brand in your target customer's mind.

19. **Delivering on Your Promises:** A benefit is a promise—would you ever make a promise to a friend that you couldn't keep? A brand promise is a mark of integrity, and creates a certain expectation of performance. Your customer wants a predictable experience, so your product must be able to deliver the brand's benefit/promise.

20. **Good Branding Never Ends:** There are several ways to communicate and leverage the essence of a brand, but there must be a corporate culture of innovation that understands the importance of a constant dialog with consumers and has a team of marketers who truly appreciate and know how to sustain an emotional connection with their customer, one that is consistent, relevant, and aspirational.

Notes

Chapter 4

1. IBM Global Chief Marketing Officer Study (2010).
2. Bronson and Merryman (2010).
3. Michalko (2011).
4. Lehrer (2012).
5. Shapiro (2012).

Chapter 5

1. Gold (2012).
2. Konrath (2005).
3. Aaker (1996).
4. IBM Global Chief Marketing Officer Study (2010).
5. Clifford (2012).
6. *Wikipedia* (2012).
7. Sinek (2010).

References

Aaker, D. A. (1996). *Building strong brands*. New York, NY: Free Press.

Bronson, P., & Merryman, A. (2010). *The creativity crisis*. Retrieved May 21, 2012, from *Newsweek*, The Daily Beast: http://www.thedailybeast.com/newsweek/2010/07/10/the-creativity-crisis.html

Clifford, S. (2012, March 27). *Knowing cost, the customer sets the price*. Retrieved May 21, 2012, from *The New York Times*: http://www.nytimes.com/2012/03/28/business/retailers-rush-to-adjust-to-price-smart-shoppers.html

Gold, C. (2012, January 5). *Getting sophisticated: What B2B tech marketers must learn from B2C*. Retrieved May 21, 2012, from MENGonline: http://www.mengonline.com/community/newsroom/meng_blend/blog/2012/01/05/getting-sophisticated-what-b2b-tech-marketers-must-learn-from-b2c

IBM Global Chief Marketing Officer Study. (2010). *From stretched to strengthened*. Retrieved May 21, 2012, from IBM: http://www-935.ibm.com/services/us/cmo/cmostudy2011/cmo-registration.html

Konrath, J. (2005). *Selling to big companies*. Chicago, IL: Dearborn Trade Pub.

Lehrer, J. (2012). *Imagine: How creativity works*. Boston, MA: Houghton Mifflin Harcourt.

Michalko, M. (2011, October 22). *Creative thinking: The seven deadly sins that prevent creative thinking*. Retrieved May 21, 2012, from Psychology Today: http://www.psychologytoday.com/blog/creative-thinkering/201110/the-seven-deadly-sins-prevent-creative-thinking

Shapiro, A. (2012, April 16). *Stop blabbing about innovation and start actually doing it*. Retrieved May 21, 2012, from Fast Company: http://www.fastcompany.com/1833190/stop-blabbing-about-innovation-and-start-actually-doing-it

Sinek, S. (2010, May). *How great leaders inspire action*. Retrieved May 24, 2012, from TEDxPugetSound: http://www.ted.com/talks/lang/en/simon_sinek_how_great_leaders_inspire_action.html

Wikipedia. (2012, May 21). *Value-based pricing*. Retrieved May 24, 2012, from Wikipedia: http://en.wikipedia.org/wiki/Value-based_pricing

Bibliography

Aaker, D. (1991). *Managing brand equity*. New York, NY: The Free Press.

Aaker, D. (1992). *Developing business strategies*. New York, NY: John Wiley & Sons.

Aaker, D., & Joachimsthaler, E. (2000). *Brand leadership*. New York, NY: The Free Press.

Arnold, D. (1992). *The handbook of brand management*. Reading, MA: Addison-Wesley.

Bedbury, S. (2002). *A new brand world*. New York, NY: The Penguin Group.

Begley, S (2002, August 26). New ABC's of branding. *Wall Street Journal*.

Bianco, A. (2004, July 11). The vanishing mass market. *Businessweek*.

Blackett, T., & Robins, R. (2001). *Brand medicine*. New York, NY: Palgrave.

Botelho, G. (2003, December). *Selling to the world*. Retrieved from CNN.com

Czerniawski, R., & Maloney, M. (1999). *Creating brand loyalty*. New York, NY: AMACOM.

Davis, S. (2002). *Brand asset management*. San Francisco, CA: Jossey-Bass (John Wiley & Sons).

Gregory, J. (1997). *Leveraging the corporate brand*. Lincolnwood, IL: NTC Business Books.

Khalap, K. (2004, April). Maintaining brand loyalty when crisis strikes. *Strategic Marketing*.

Laitin, J. (2004, May). Does branding work in pharmaceutical marketing? *Ingenta OTC Branding*.

Lasswell, M. (2004, August). Lost in translation. *Business 2.0*.

Levine, M. (2003). *A branded world*. New York, NY: John Wiley & Sons.

Nedobity, W. (2002, September). *A name to license*. Retrieved from Knowledge-Finder.com

Pmlive.com (2004, September). *Building brands*.

Pmlive.com (2004, September 22). *Looking for the perfect relationship?*

Prahalad, D. (2011, December 8). Why trust matters more than ever for brands. *Harvard Business Review*.

Ribbink, K. (2003, July). Corporate branding. *Pharma Voice*.

Ries, A. (1996). *Focus*. New York, NY: Harper Business.

Roll, M. (2004). Perspectives on corporate branding strategy. *VentureRepublic*.

Surowiecki, J. (2004, November). The decline of brands. *Wired Magazine*.

Travis, D. (2000). *Emotional branding*. Roseville, CA: Prima Venture.

Treistman, J. (2004, September). Branding the product. *RoperASW*.

Upshaw, L. (1995). *Building brand identity*. New York, NY: John Wiley & Sons.

Index